HOW TO ORGANIZE AND MANAGE A SEMINAR

What to Do and When to Do It

Sheila L. Murray

A SPECTRUM BOOK

PRENTICE-HALL, INC., Englewood Cliffs, N.J. 07632

Library of Congress Cataloging in Publication Data

Murray, Sheila L., date.
How to organize and manage a seminar.

"A Spectrum Book."
Includes index.
1. Congresses and conventions—Handbooks,
manuals, etc.   2. Meetings—Handbooks, manuals,
etc.   3. Seminars—Handbooks, manuals, etc.
I. Title.
AS6.M87   658.4'563   82-5381
ISBN 0-13-425199-7   AACR2
ISBN 0-13-425181-4 (pbk.)

DEDICATED TO
my mother, Julia Stribley,
who taught me persistence
and the ability to dream big dreams,
and
Cavett Robert, my speaking mentor—
a genius of our time.

This book is available at a special discount when ordered
in large quantities. Contact Prentice-Hall, Inc., General Publishing Division,
Special Sales, Englewood Cliffs, N.J. 07632.

Editorial/production supervision: Marlys Lehmann
Manufacturing buyer: Cathie Lenard

ISBN 0-13-425199-7

ISBN 0-13-425181-4 {PBK.}

Prentice-Hall International, Inc., *London*
Prentice-Hall of Australia Pty. Limited, *Sydney*
Prentice-Hall Canada Inc., *Toronto*
Prentice-Hall of India Private Limited, *New Delhi*
Prentice-Hall of Japan, Inc., *Tokyo*
Prentice-Hall of Southeast Asia Pte. Ltd., *Singapore*
Whitehall Books Limited, *Wellington, New Zealand*
Editora Prentice-Hall do Brasil Ltda., *Rio de Janeiro*

CONTENTS

IV
THE SEMINAR

V
EVALUATION, FOLLOW-UP, AND DEBRIEFING

PREFACE

Why This Book Was Written

We live in an age of instant everything. In recent years a new "instant education" form has emerged. It is challenging the traditional, time-consuming, academic classroom learning. The new form is called the *seminar, (workshop, clinic, conference)*. Now, in a day or two or three you can become an instant expert on just about any subject—from learning how to make a million dollars (in your spare time) to running a large corporation (full-time, one presumes).

With the growth of this new seminar industry, there is an increasing need for information on all facets of conducting seminars. Many companies and seminar leaders have expressed a great deal of interest in acquiring a manual/workbook/guide to assist them in making the most of the staging and logistics of seminars. That's what this book is all about.

Who Would Use This Book?

The variety and number of individuals or groups that would make use of this book increases daily. There is amazing growth in the seminar concept of learning in both public seminars and within groups and organizations.

Any group or person who is involved in sharing information in a seminar situation and must maximize the use of time would use this book. For example: individuals who conduct public seminars, meeting planners, companies and corporations—large and small, nonprofit groups, and service groups. The list is endless.

So, if you are looking for ways to conduct more effective seminars, workshops, meetings, conferences, or clinics, you've come to the right place.

How to Use This Book

This book was designed to give you a chronological frame of reference for your seminar (as opposed to just subject matter).

In fifteen years of being involved with seminars, I have seen more mistakes and problems arise from people not knowing *when* to do something than from not knowing *what* to do.

The *"what* to do's" (subject matter) are all covered in detail. But they are covered in *"when* to" (chronological) order.

An example would be:

SPEAKER/TRAINER (S/T)

Sections II and IV both have information regarding your S/T.

Section II—Advance Work:

Tells you the "what to's" and "how to's" of working with your S/T before the seminar.

Section IV—The Seminar:

Discusses the "what to's" and "how to's" of working with your S/T on the day(s) of the seminar(s).

So, whether you use this book as a reference source, planning guide, working manual, or problem-solving tool, you will save time, money, and effort by thinking of and planning your seminar in chronological order.

Keep in Mind

If you are new to the job of seminar planning, you may say, "But I don't have any previous experience in planning or implementing a seminar!" That may be true. However, you have probably been to a seminar, a meeting, a conference, a group function. It is practically impossible to grow up and work in America and *not* attend some kind of meeting (we Americans are very meeting prone). So, look back—what do you think made the function successful or unsuccessful? What kind of facility was it held in? What can you remember about how you felt? How was the room set? Did you like what refreshments were served at the break? What did you see that you would change?

Turn to the Contents page and notice the subjects you already know about. Odds are you know and have opinions on much more than you realize.

As you attend other seminars, make notes of what you see, hear, and feel. Then bring the ideas back and translate them into actions and plans for your seminar.

ACKNOWLEDGMENTS

The words *thank you* are so inadequate when it comes to thanking and acknowledging those who have helped, encouraged, and supported me during the writing of this book.

I would be remiss if I did not thank all my clients in the United States and Canada, for without them I would not have experienced or developed the expertise to write this book.

This book would not have become a reality without the unending support and fine work of my right arm and assistant, Irene Brown. Ellen Soffette put in many long hours typing and retyping. I thank her and Judy Lofton for their excellence at the typewriter and their willingness to help.

I would also like to thank all the people who allowed me to interview them for the sections ASK A PRO. They are indeed professionals and I am most appreciative of their time and thoughts. .

My two mentors, Og Mandino (my writing mentor) and Cavett Robert (my speaking mentor), have both given me immeasurable encouragement and inspiration. Thank you, Og and Cavett.

My sons, Mike and Shannon, have always been among my greatest reasons for achieving any goal, this book included.

The idea for this book was born on an important January evening. For this I thank my then friend, and now husband, Bill Bethel.

Professional speaker/trainer **SHEILA MURRAY** is an author and the originator of the "Getting Control" series of speeches and seminars. She is founder and president of Getting Control, Inc., a San Francisco-based marketing and training corporation. Prior to becoming a professional speaker she was an award-winning salesperson and manager. Ms. Murray is listed in the 1981 edition of *Who's Who of American Women,* and enjoys the reputation of being one of today's most successful platform speakers.

FOREWORD

How many times have you attended a meeting where the mike doesn't function, or the coffee fails to arrive at the scheduled break, or the room arrangement inhibits group discussion? These are just a few of the concerns that face anyone in charge of a seminar. Details, to be sure. But details can be the critical factors in the success of a meeting.

Staging and logistics can make or break a seminar. That is why I am pleased to see a book devoted to that topic. From my experience at Xerox Learning Systems, I've found that the importance of planning can never be stressed too much. Sheila Murray looks into every aspect and gives both the experienced meeting planner and the neophyte a thorough checklist of details for a successful meeting: how to plan, budget, and schedule a seminar; how to obtain a speaker or trainer and what they need to make an effective presentation. She also provides an analysis of various audiovisual techniques and equipment, tells how to arrange the room depending on the objectives and group size, and describes how to make travel arrangements and review facility requirements, including fire protection.

But that's just the beginning. *How to Organize and Manage a Seminar* also tells how to communicate with participants, the ins and outs of registration and running the actual meeting, and how to obtain objective feedback.

This book takes you every step of the way from preplanning to final evaluation. In summary, it helps you anticipate the unexpected and plan for almost any eventuality.

S.E. Sanderson, Jr.
President, Xerox Learning Systems

part one

BEFORE YOU BEGIN

chapter one
TAKE TIME TO PLAN

"Let's put on a seminar." That sentence can lead to either gray hair and ulcers or smiles and excitement about "next time."

What you do in the very beginning stages of planning will have a major effect on the success or failure of your seminar.

In the past fifteen years I have attended some wonderful seminars, which made me glad I had spent the time, money, and effort to attend. Then there were those that made me think that the quote, "Fools rush in where angels fear to tread," was written for some seminar planners.

Among the seminars that were crashing failures and those just less than successful I soon noticed a common factor—lack of detailed planning. In the mid-sixties, when I began planning and conducting seminars, I succumbed to the same temptation—neglect of detailed planning. I soon learned the hard way that advance, detailed planning was well worth the time and effort.

Do yourself the biggest favor possible in relation to seminar planning. Now, at the very beginning, immediately after your decision to put on a seminar, go to your calendar and schedule an initial planning session. A brainstorming-mastermind session.

Gather together the key individuals who will be involved in the seminar. Set as much time aside as possible, at least several hours. Meet at a location that is free of distraction and interruptions.

Each person should bring two lists. The first is a list of the key ideas, concepts, objectives, and questions related to the seminar. The second list should be what each person feels are his or her talents and/or skills in the planning and implementation of the seminar (as far as each can tell, at this point; reassessments can be made later).

For example, someone may feel he or she is good at budgeting or at making graphs and charts to track the stages of planning. Someone else may feel they have creative-thinking talents or administrative skills.

At this point you are just looking for general abilities. Assigning tasks and jobs will come later.

With your lists in hand, discuss generally how each member sees the finished product, the completed seminar. Then write a collective description of the seminar as if it were finished and everything went perfectly. Pretend that there were no delays, there was perfect attendance, the speaker/trainer was great, the location perfect—nothing went wrong.

Now that you have the perfect seminar described and anticipated, you can begin creating your game plan.

Just as the coach of a winning team will mentally picture victory, even before the contest, the game would never be played without a detailed game plan. Play by play, the plan is rehearsed and practiced until the players know it by heart and react automatically.

It is now time for *you* to start a detailed game plan, to begin anticipating the problems and solutions. Game plans always require adjustments along the way. Yours will too. But the middle of the game (seminar) is no time to change the entire plan. So always plan for the ideal seminar. High expectations will result in a much more successful seminar. Then be ready for the unexpected problems or changes that will occur. You'll be able to make the adjustments more easily if you have a well-planned, detailed, basic game plan.

chapter two
THE SEMINAR PLANNING TRIANGLE

At the first two planning meetings the primary concerns are:

1. To develop the seminar theme and objectives.
2. To outline a profile of the seminar participants.
3. To develop the seminar format and design, in general.
4. To develop the staging and logistics strategy.

The success of your seminar will depend on the congruity of these four aspects of seminar planning.

THEME AND OBJECTIVES

Planning a seminar is different from planning a general meeting, conference, or convention in one major aspect—that of theme and objectives. (A seminar can be the entire function or part of a larger event, meeting, conference, or convention.)

When a person or group of people decide to conduct a seminar, they usually have a need to fill or subject matter in mind, which establishes the general theme and objectives.

It will be helpful to define these two words, *theme* and *objectives*.

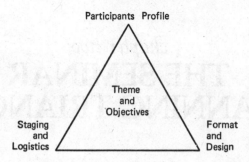

SEMINAR PLANNING TRIANGLE

Participants Profile

Theme and Objectives

Staging and Logistics

Format and Design

Theme: The theme is the general purpose of the seminar. It helps establish the objectives. It sets the climate and atmosphere for the seminar.

Objectives: The objectives of the seminar are, clearly stated, specific benefits. These benefits accrue to both the seminar participants and the sponsor.

In these first meetings your seminar theme and objectives must be defined and outlined. This may be done by the seminar coordinator or by the planning team.

These clearly defined objectives will:

1. Determine the type of participants best suited for the seminar.
2. Help you decide on the format and design of the seminar.
3. Give direction to the "what to," "how to," and "when to" of the staging and logistics.

A detailed set of seminar objectives is like the following goal-setting quote: "If you don't know where you are going, how will you know when you get there?"

PARTICIPANTS' PROFILE

The profile of seminar participants should come from a consensus of your seminar planning staff.

Regardless of the simplicity or complexity of the seminar objectives, you don't want to miss important information about the participants or make erroneous assumptions about them that will affect the results of the seminar.

Here are some factors to consider:

1. What information do you have on the socioeconomic and educational background of the participants? Do you need additional information? How will this information affect the seminar results? Example: Your seminar participants will be people who have not had a college education. They have worked their way up from a production plant job to a supervisory position. They are of mixed ages, ethnic, and socioeconomic backgrounds. They have been in this new position just long enough to have some "hands-on" experience, but they have had no formal supervisory training. The objective of the seminar is to give them some basic supervisory training. You can see that the more you know about this group, the better able you will be to design the seminar and meet their expectations and yours.

2. You may wish to find out what other seminars the participants have attended in either your seminar subject area or related areas.

   It is also helpful to know what other seminars are available on your subject matter. This information can be obtained from researching trade journals or other publications that appeal to your type of participants. An information-gathering questionnaire to your seminar participants can include specific questions about their past seminar experience, and what others they would be interested in attending.　•

3. Establishing expectations is very important. In the questionnaire mentioned above, you can ask what the participants want to know, learn, or experience. Questions about where they have attended previous seminars, for example, could be quite revealing. If they have attended only in-house training sessions (in a company training room), and you are taking them out of town for a two-day seminar at a resort facility, this will certainly affect their expectations.

4. Another factor to consider is that groups of people often take on a personality that is a composite of their individual personalities.

   How might this affect your seminar? In the previous example of taking a group to a resort area, the result may be a more relaxed atmosphere than you desire. Certainly, the area itself will affect them, but the personality change that occurs at a resort facility, as opposed to what they are used to in the restricted corporate structure, can greatly affect the seminar.

   A group personality is not necessarily bad, you just need to be aware of it.

This book is primarily written about the staging and logistics of seminars, and certainly, this is a very important part of a successful seminar.

But if you don't have a complete profile of your seminar participants, you can miss your objectives by a mile, your design and format can be inappropriate, or you can have an inappropriate speaker/trainer conduct the seminar. Any one of these can spell disaster for your seminar. The participant profile is as important a part of the Seminar Planning Triangle as the other three components.

FORMAT AND DESIGN

The format and design of the seminar are the "what" and "how" of the seminar itself.

What information will be transmitted during the seminar, and how will this be accomplished?

There are expectations on both sides, yours and the participants'. In the previous section participants' expectations were mentioned: what they expect to learn, improve, or experience and how they can expect to accomplish this. Your format and design play a critical part in these expectations.

A group of first-time seminar attendees may have much less experience in group participation and not know what to expect. So if group activities are in your design, you need to allow for this with explicit explanation and the allotment of extra time to finish the activity.

There are expectations that you have regarding participants' interaction, response, and results. To meet both sets of expectations there are several factors to consider in planning your format and design.

1. Subcultures and Group Personalities

The factor of group personality comes into consideration again. For example, if you have a group of participants who are normally of the less assertive type, you may need to have material or exercises that can bring them out, exercises that give them the desire and power to express themselves. At this point you may also need some backup material and ideas to control the group. I've seen seminars where the speaker/trainer lost control of a group of nonassertive types when they found their collective power. The design and format was not flexible enough to adjust to their response.

2. Learning Curve

People assimilate ideas and material at different rates during the day. The learning curve of a seminar refers to this.

From 8 A.M. until noon most people seem to be more responsive, learn quicker, and retain more. After lunch the ratio drops; in the evening it drops even more. What does this mean? It means that in your seminar format and design you need to consider the seriousness of the material and the mental agility necessary to assimilate it and learn.

What device will you use to lighten the mental load? Will you take a refreshment break? Will you relieve the heavy material with fun exercises? After lunch, do you plan to have lighter material and ideas to work with? When will you have an afternoon break? Can you have material continuity and still change the pace?

If your seminar goes into the evening, what will the format be? Discussion groups work well in the evening. Short sessions with several breaks also work well.

As you attend or conduct seminars, track the learning curve of the participants. You will be able to detect patterns and clues as to how best to plan the flow of your seminars.

3. Depth and Amount of Material

Nonstop dissemination of new or heavy material can overdose the mind. The participants are listening but not learning. You may find it necessary to design the seminar for more than one session.

The format and design should be structured so that the information and material flows easily and comfortably. In other words, don't try to cover more material than there is time for. Leave time for participation, reaction, digestion of materials, question-and-answer periods, and group discussion.

4. Format and Design

Format and design are related to staging and logistics and play a very important role.

For example, if you are planning a high-technology seminar or an intense learning experience, a cruise ship will not do.

The registration area and refreshment breaks can be used quite effectively to set the stage, create atmosphere, change the pace, lighten or increase enthusiasm and activity.

As you work with the other ideas in this book you will find numerous suggestions on how you can integrate your format and design with staging and logistics to create a dynamic, well-received seminar.

If, however, you feel you need assistance in developing your format or design, there are professionals who can help. In Section VI—Where Else Can I Get Help, under Resources there is a list of organizations and associations that can help you find the person or company you need.

STAGING AND LOGISTICS

A successful seminar consists of equal research, planning, and execution of the ideas and actions in all four areas of the Seminar Planning Triangle.

The information contained in the rest of this book will give you the "what to" and "when to" tasks of staging and logistics. They will be affected by the three other major factors. All four play an integral part in your seminar.

As you conduct your first planning meetings, step back and view your seminar from a participant's viewpoint. Put yourself in his or her place. How will the four major aspects affect the response to and results from the seminar? Viewing the seminar in this way will make a major difference in the outcome.

Remember that there is no perfect seminar. You'll make mistakes or see things that you will change next time. Your knowledge and experience will grow with each seminar you plan and conduct. Keep an open mind and don't be afraid to try new and innovative ideas. Happy Seminaring!

chapter three

TRACKING YOUR SEMINAR

The way to accomplish a successful seminar is to track your thoughts, decisions, actions and results.

Before your second meeting you will need to have the beginnings of a written plan. You may want to have each member of the group prepare a plan of action, as he or she sees it. Then, at your second meeting, you combine the ideas and develop the master plan.

THE TRAIN TO SUCCESS

In looking at the overall game plan of your seminar, it will be helpful if you keep this picture in mind: Your seminar is a train going down a track. The tracks are laid out in chronological order. If the train derails or stops, it is because a section of the track has been left out or not laid correctly. Just as the train can't travel down an incomplete track, your seminar cannot finish successfully without each of the major sections being well planned and executed.

SEMINAR FLOW CHART

Each of the categories in the illustration will run more smoothly if you develop an overall master flow chart to track them with. In the begin-

11

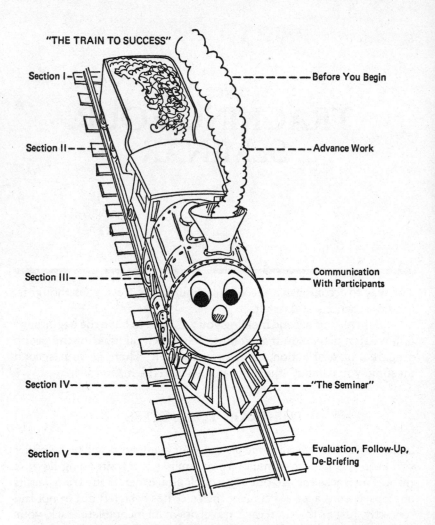

"THE TRAIN TO SUCCESS"

Section I — Before You Begin

Section II — Advance Work

Section III — Communication With Participants

Section IV — "The Seminar"

Section V — Evaluation, Follow-Up, De-Briefing

ning, use a large piece of paper (perhaps a flip chart) so there is room to add components as they come along. Keep it posted somewhere in full view and within easy reach for notations.

Allow as much time as possible for each component of the flow chart to be completed.

In establishing the start and finish dates of these components, consult the people involved. How long do they think it will take to get the job done? If you are responsible for the task, use the "who, what, when, where, and why" thinking method to arrive at your time frame. When deciding on any finish date, add a day or two for good measure. Everything takes longer than planned.

In deciding time frames it will help to review the survey or postseminar questionnaire sent to the participants of the previous seminar (if you had one).

If you have not had a previous seminar or did not do a follow-up mailing, you should plan one for this seminar. Among the evaluation/ follow-up questions you need to include those that ask for opinions and suggestions related to time frames allotted for participants' responses, such as sending in registration money and/or information.

Later in this book you will find further information regarding follow-up questionnaires, questions to ask for improving the next seminar.

If you are coordinator you may want to have a private flow chart with three "finish dates" for each component:

1. The date on which you would like to have the task finished, usually later than the posted date. Give yourself some "rush time" if necessary.
2. The posted date for those involved to shoot for, usually earlier than date #1.
3. The "drop-dead date"—the absolute, must-be-done, final, final date. This date will tell you when to hit the panic button. Let's hope you never have to do that, but you need to know when that date is.

An example of early-planning time frames would be the booking of a facility for the seminar. If the seminar is to be held in a metropolitan area where hotel and other facilities are popular, you may need to reserve the rooms months or even years in advance. The same may be true of a small town or suburban area where appropriate facilities are limited and therefore in great demand.

From an overall viewpoint, the advance work on your flow chart and the time frames involved will be an asset or a liability, depending on how thoroughly you approach that task.

It is better to have too much time and create a lag period in your preparations and arrangements than to have that nerve-shattering last-minute race with the clock.

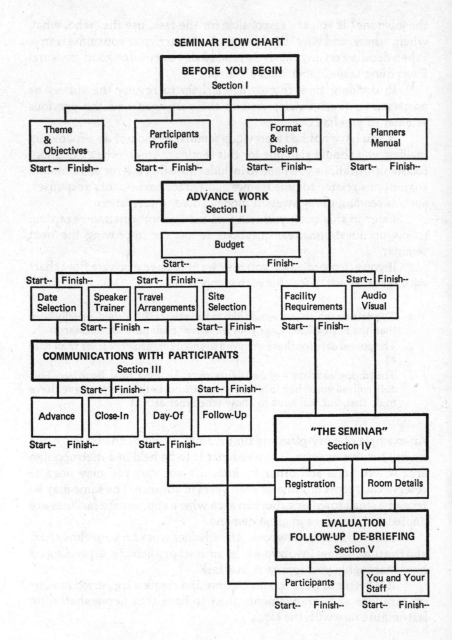

SEMINAR FLOW CHART

BEFORE YOU BEGIN
Section I

Theme & Objectives	Participants Profile	Format & Design	Planners Manual
Start-- Finish--	Start-- Finish--	Start-- Finish--	Start-- Finish--

ADVANCE WORK
Section II

Budget
Start-- Finish--

Start-- Finish--   Start-- Finish--   Start-- Finish--

Date Selection	Speaker Trainer	Travel Arrangements	Site Selection	Facility Requirements	Audio Visual

Start-- Finish--   Start-- Finish--   Start-- Finish--

COMMUNICATIONS WITH PARTICIPANTS
Section III

Start-- Finish--   Start-- Finish--

Advance	Close-In	Day-Of	Follow-Up

Start-- Finish--   Start-- Finish--

"THE SEMINAR"
Section IV

Registration	Room Details

EVALUATION FOLLOW-UP DE-BRIEFING
Section V

Participants	You and Your Staff
Start-- Finish--	Start-- Finish--

14

An important concept is to have start and finish dates marked clearly at each box (see sample). As soon as you feel you have a sufficiently general flow chart for the overall seminar, make copies and distribute them to each member of the seminar team.

It may be helpful to give it to, or at least show it to, your suppliers when you begin working with them. It will assist them in understanding your objectives and time frames.

MASTER CHECKLIST

Now that you have a flow chart, the next step is to use the master checklist (see sample). The purpose of the flow chart is to have a general pattern of the tasks to be done—the objectives to be reached. The master checklist gives you the tool with which to define and assign the details connected with each of the flow-chart boxes.

The form is very basic in design. The value is in its simplicity and versatility. The variety and complexity of its use is up to you. It can be used to track a series of large tasks or to break them into smaller sections. It can also be used to assign a person several tasks, tracking the progress on one standard form. The checklists are communication vehicles. They can be sent back and forth to committee members working on similar or opposite tasks. They can update everyone on the progress of the entire seminar, or on any single part.

As soon as you begin using the master checklist, set up a file or binder to keep a central control for all checklists being used. You will note that on the bottom of the form there is a space for "Copies To:"—one should always be included in the planner's manual. At any time, the seminar coordinator can track who is doing what, when, and where by referring to the planner's manual.

The art of planning and implementing a seminar is a series of decisions. Some will be based on your past experience and knowledge. Other decisions will be made on projections and expectations. The flow chart and checklists will be invaluable in your decision-making process during this seminar and as a research tool for any other seminars you may be involved with in the future. You will also need them in your debriefing session after the seminar.

TO:_____FROM:_____DATE:_____

TASK OR JOB TITLE:_____				
DATE	TIME	PLACE	PERSON/S	DESCRIPTION OF TASK OR FUNCTION

SPECIAL REMARKS/INSTRUCTIONS:

COPIES TO: _____

The more time spent in the beginning sessions, the fewer large problems you will have along the way. There is no such thing as a perfect seminar. There will always be something you would change or do differently, if you could do it over again. However, attention to detail is the key. There will always be surprises and problems that arise. But your detailed planning will help to eliminate many of these possible problems and lessen the severity of others. It is worth the time and trouble to take the time to plan.

Ask a Pro

Interview with:
Mr. Cavett Robert
Founder, NATIONAL SPEAKERS ASSOCIATION
Phoenix, Arizona

SHEILA: What advice would you give to someone new to the job of staging seminars?

CAVETT: To someone new I would say, "If you want to study law, go to law school. If you want to study seminars, use O.P.E. (other peoples' experience)."

Don't try to learn through trial and error. You won't live long enough to learn all you need to know. Engineers don't reinvent the wheel every generation. Find a person, or people, who have had experience in conducting seminars and learn from them.

SHEILA: Is there a single most important item in staging a seminar?

CAVETT: The most important item in conducting a seminar is, Know your audience. Start where they are, not where you are. Find out who they are, how long have they been in their field, etcetera.

Know what time of day you're going to speak. Groups have personalities, just like individuals. Different groups have different responses. A morning group will have a different response than an evening group. In the morning you can use seventy-five percent good, deep material with a lot of substance and twenty-five percent humor. At night it is the reverse.

If you are speaking to a convention and you are the opening speaker, you would certainly not make the same kind of a speech as the closing speaker. If you are the closing speaker, try to sit in on the other speeches. You should try to tie the ideas together and challenge the audience to use all the ideas presented. Tell them what to do about what they learned.

SHEILA: In staging seminars, what do you think is the most common mistake?

CAVETT: The answer to your second question—not paying attention to your audience, not knowing them.

Meeting planners will be delighted to have you contact them about all the details and information regarding their group. The mistake is in not doing detailed research and then tailoring the speech or seminar for them. Find out any special information you can about their especial interests. Let them know that you care enough about them to find out what's going on in their world. Do they have a theme for that certain event, conference, convention? Find out, refer to it. As I said in question two, know your audience.

17

SHEILA: Do you have a final comment?

CAVETT: As a seminar speaker/trainer, the commitment to improve peoples' lives is most important. Lose yourself in your message. Forget about what a great speaker you are—help people fulfill their dreams and ambitions. Seek this kind of fulfillment as a speaker/trainer, not just recognition. Have a love affair with your audience—give them all you've got.

Try to improve and learn your craft a little better with each presentation you make. School is never out for a professional. Keep your seminar ideas and material up to date. Have the gift of dissatisfaction and divine discontent; always look for new and better ways to present your material.

The answer to success is the mentor system. Find someone who will help you and learn all you can from them. Then share what you know with someone else—it will form a chain of information and success.

chapter four
PLANNER'S MANUAL

In planning and implementing a seminar, whether there are ten or one thousand participants, someone must oversee the entire project. Whoever that person is, he or she must have a manual or guide to track the seminar from inception through postseminar debriefing.

We have already discussed flow charts and checklists. I have suggested that a central file be set up where copies of all the checklists are kept. This file is a central source of information and communication between the tasks involved and the people performing them.

A planner's manual (sometimes called a coordinator's guide or administrator's manual) entails much more than this central file. It is a compendium of all parts of the seminar. Here is the design I have found works best:

1. Using the "train to success" and your master flow chart, determine all the major seminar component areas to be completed. The planner's manual covers the entire seminar—both sides of the "train to success," not just staging and logistics.
2. Using a large three-ring binder, divide the major sections and tab them along the vertical edge, so that they can be easily distinguished.
3. The first section should contain:
   A. a copy of the master flow chart;
   B. a written description of the seminar theme, objectives, and purpose;

    C. a list of who is responsible for what;

    D. a list of all your staff members or aides, including their addresses and phone numbers.

4. Each section then follows, in order, the tasks to be completed, beginning with budget and advance work through the debriefing section and/or a section on final reports to superiors, if necessary.

5. Each tabbed section should contain:

    A. a flow chart of that section;

    B. a master checklist for that section;

    C. documentation for everything that happens regarding that section. Staff working on the section should provide information at regular intervals on everything that occurs—copies of letters, checklists, contracts, orders to suppliers. A quick summary of the day or week in a "memo to file" form should be in this section, covering such things as meetings, conversations, decisions, ideas, observations, and opinions.

At the conclusion of the seminar, the planner's manual should include final reports, follow-through and debriefing notes, and suggestions for subsequent seminars.

When the seminar is over and you are sitting in a debriefing session, you, as seminar coordinator, should be able to take the planner's manual and cover every single detail.

The sections in your manual should be duplicates of what each staff member kept throughout the entire planning and implementation process.

This does not mean that you must review each piece of paper that comes into the planner's manual along the way. However, it is crucial for you to be able to pick up that manual and know exactly who is doing what, when, where, and why. The buck stops with you. That is why you want the staff to supply any and all information along the way. You must be prepared to solve problems and make decisions. A complete planner's manual will enable you to act quickly and accurately when necessary.

In your debriefing session(s) you will be able to make an infinitely more accurate evaluation with a complete planner's manual. You will be also able to use it as a training manual or a guide for further seminars you are involved with. As your skill in seminar planning and implementation grows, so will your planner's manual. It is an invaluable tool.

chapter five
MENTORS

Webster's Dictionary: Mentor

1. Wise adviser
2. Teacher or coach

During my first years of planning and conducting seminars, the most important factor in my success was the wisdom and experience of my mentor.

It would have taken years of research and experience to acquire all the minute details involved in successful seminaring. Instead, I cut my learning time by at least one half through the training of my mentors.

Cavett Robert, the dean of professional speaking and founder of the National Speakers' Association, originated the quote, "O.P.E." (Other People's Experience). That's what the mentor-protégé relationship is based upon: other people's experience.

I've found that most people who have become successful in life and/or business are proud to share their knowledge and experience. If you find someone who can act as your mentor, it would be a wonderful experience for both of you.

I now act as a mentor for several people. Having discussed mentorship with several friends who are also mentors, we have agreed that there are some tips on the mentor-protégé relationship that would be helpful to pass on. I have listed them in the hopes that you can make the most of one of the best resources available to you—a mentor!

1. As defined by Webster's, a mentor is an adviser, coach/teacher—not a partner or replacement for your active participation. Look upon your mentor as a source of inspiration and information, not a replacement for action.

2. Be very careful of your mentor's time. The quickest way to alienate a mentor is to be on the telephone or in his or her office for repeated information and unimportant details. On the other hand, don't be afraid to ask what you may think is a dumb question. If it is a new situation or problem that has arisen, there are no dumb questions. If you have already covered the material or problem and you still have questions, make sure you aren't just being lazy. If you do need further clarification and help, then certainly contact your mentor.

3. When working with a mentor—whether in person, on the telephone, or by mail—take careful notes so you don't have to go back for repeated information. Always take notes; they will help you in preparing intelligent, meaningful questions and in retaining the information.

4. If you are asking advice of a mentor—take it! Protégés, in their enthusiasm, often ask advice and then argue the point. Don't reinvent the wheel.

5. When you receive advice and suggestions from your mentor, report back on the results or action taken. Your mentor may see that you need a slight adjustment or correction. Small game-plan refinements can be extremely helpful. If you are proceeding correctly and all is well, you need to know that also. Reporting to your mentor will give you this knowledge.

6. Once you have had a mentor, pass on the legacy. Be a mentor. It is a wonderful and rewarding endeavor.

O.P.E.—Other People's Experience—is a key to successful seminaring.

Planning and conducting a seminar can be a fun, exciting project. This book was written to give you a basic detailed plan to work from. Expand on it, be creative, develop your own style, and most of all, have fun!

Ask a Pro

Interview with:
Mr. S.E. Sanderson, Jr.
President, XEROX LEARNING SYSTEMS
Stamford, Connecticut

SHEILA: What advice would you give to someone new to the job of staging seminars?

STAN: The first thing we do at Xerox is have the person understand the expectations of the participants and really get to know the materials that will be presented. We then put them through the seminar to understand it as a participant. Next, we have them co-administer a seminar, and then we have them run one of their own. This method is not only to have them understand the materials, but also to understand all the little ancillary things that make the seminar vital. That includes the audiovisual aids, charts, books, and the facilities themselves. It is very, very important that the seminar administrator check out all of the details in advance before the seminar itself. Be sure that everything is ready to go and works when the seminar is conducted. It's something that you really can't delegate to a hotel staff member.

SHEILA: Is there a single most important item in staging a seminar?

STAN: Probably the most critical thing is the administrative preparation—understanding the materials to be presented, understanding the participants and their expectations.

Secondly, the site selection: Is it a convenient location and is the facility adequate? We find many times that a seminar administrator may use a facility simply on the recommendation of someone else and not really check out all of the details, for example, the lighting or the air conditioning.

The third thing is the scheduling during the seminar—where things are supposed to go and what time they're supposed to arrive. This all should be worked out during the advance work: materials, aids, schedules, etcetera.

SHEILA: In staging seminars, what do you think is the most common mistake?

STAN: Again, one of the most common mistakes is the seminar administrator not understanding the intent of the seminar itself. When it comes to logistics, the faux pas that happen when the equipment doesn't work, when the flip charts don't seem to arrive, when the tape recorder isn't there, when the bulb blows out and is not replaced because there is no secondary bulb—those annoying things happen so often simply because the seminar leader or administrator was not prepared.

SHEILA: Do you have a final comment?

STAN: In reference to staging and logistics, my final comment would be just don't take anything for granted. Don't assume that things are going to be done the way you want them to be done. Make sure that you check them out in advance.

part two
ADVANCE WORK

chapter six
BUDGET

The first topic of advance work is your seminar budget. The first projections will quite often be "guesstimates," but you have to start somewhere. Many expenses are overlooked in the beginning stages of planning, not on purpose, but rather from a lack of experience.

As your plans become firm you can zero in on actual costs. Budget overruns and loss of profits come from unforeseen expenses. You can't always predict these expenses, but you can be aware of the items involved in conducting seminars.

Here is a checklist. Your specific needs, such as audiovisual equipment, will add to this list. You'll notice that a space for Due Date is given. You don't want any budget surprises. Keeping the due date firmly in mind will help with the cash outlay and help you avoid surprises.

Budget Checklist

Item	Cost	Due Date
1. Planner's Manual		
2. Planning and Debriefing Meeting: Time away from job Location		

Item	Cost	Due Date
3. On-Site Inspection:		
Travel expenses		
Lodging		
Time away from job cost		
4. Audiovisual:		
Microphones, etc.		
5. Speaker/Trainer:		
Speaking Fees		
Preparation time charges		
Travel		
Lodging		
Miscellaneous		
6. Food and Beverage:		
Eye-opener		
Morning break		
Lunch		
Afternoon break		
Evening meal		
Evening snack		
Deposits		
Gratuities		
7. Travel and Lodging:		
Staff and/or participant		
Air fare		
Car rentals		
Lodging		
Meals		
Miscellaneous		
8. Facility Rooms:		
Overnight		
Seminar		
Luncheon		
Breakout		
Deposits		
Gratuities		
9. Printing:		
Brochures/announcements		
Workbook/handouts		
Participants' questionnaires		
10. Photographer		
11. Handy Dandy Scout Box		

Item	Cost	Due Date
12. Permits		
13. Shipping:		
Printed matter		
Equipment		
14. Part-time staff		
15. Miscellaneous:		
Postage		
Telephone		
Secretarial		

Using this checklist will enable you to be far more efficient at budget projections. It will also affect your marketing endeavors if you are planning a public seminar. You may find that your fees are too low, or that you need to rework your budget to stay within the cost already projected (and reflected in the participants' fees).

Some other budget factors to keep in mind are areas that are unique to your seminar. There may be special areas of concern where normal budget appropriations will increase in unusual proportions to your group. For example, if you are having a group of VIP's attend your two-day seminar, you may want to upgrade their sleeping accommodations. Make a separate list of these types of expenses; then, to be sure your figures are accurate, consult whomever you need to before including them in the overall budget.

If you have in-house facilities that can do the same job as an outside supplier, break down the direct and indirect costs. Compare them to one another. It may be cost-effective to have an outside supplier do the job, one that specializes in that area and can bring the job in on time, in exactly the way you want it done. In-house facilities can get bogged down when they do work for several departments or people at the same time.

If your seminar is being planned in advance for a future date (more than a few months away), you need to estimate any possible rise in costs. For example, if you are budgeting air fares to transport the participants from your company to the seminar location, you will surely go over budget if you are not careful. For someone planning a public seminar, the same can hold true for your participants. This may then affect attendance if the participants are paying for their own transportation. These anticipated rises in cost cannot be accounted for to the penny, but they need to be examined.

Be very detailed and specific on every item included in your budget. Then calculate the amount you can afford to use as a miscellaneous fund for emergencies.

The importance of any seminar is, of course, the successful transfer of knowledge and information. However, the realities of the bottom line must always be kept in the forefront of your planning.

Budget cutting is never an easy task, nor a pleasant one. But if you have to cut your budget, do it in the beginning, as soon as you see that overruns are imminent. It is easier to move funds from one area or part of the seminar budget to another in the early stages of planning.

chapter seven
DATE SELECTION

The selection of a date or dates for your seminar depends upon the subjects covered in your "advance work": budget, facility requirements, travel arrangements, and speaker/trainer schedule.

Before beginning the selection process of a seminar date, review these subjects. Gather your committee or staff together and (if you have not done so already) assign these subjects to different people (use the checklist). Each person should research the ideas, problems, and requirements associated with their task. After this research is completed, a meeting should be held to review the ramifications of the date selection upon each of the subjects and vice versa.

Whoever is in charge of date selection should be aware of the additional following considerations:

- Review the past participants' comments on your postseminar survey (follow-up questionnaire) for feedback on date selections.
- Choosing a date that allows you to take advantage of off-season rates at facilities has both a positive and negative side. The positive side consists of the financial saving(s) available. Many facilities make it very attractive to hold a seminar at their location during the off-season. The negative side is the image you wish to impart to your participants. A seminar during the off-season will not always put you in the best light. In warm-climate areas, participants may not appreciate the savings when they suffer discomfort from the heat. Weather versus comfort may be a very important consideration.

- The summer months are often a very good time to have a seminar. Many industries slow down during these months in anticipation of increased fall production. If you are planning an in-house seminar, this may be an important consideration. Putting on a public seminar may be just the opposite. Summer months are traditional vacation times, and people may not be available to attend. If they are taking vacation time, they may not be willing or able to take extra time away from their work to attend your seminar. With children out of school, time availabilities change for people with families.

Conducting Multiple Seminars

If you plan to market or conduct the same seminar in different cities at different times of the year, it is usually to do one of two things: to increase attendance or to increase profits. Before doing so, consider these factors:

1. Is it really helpful to have different times available for the same seminar? Or does it cause people to procrastinate or become confused about making a decision on which date to attend?
2. How are participants' personal expenses affected? Must they travel, and if so, what costs are incurred?
3. Are the time variations really advantageous? If so, to whom and why?
4. Will offering the same seminar in different locations really increase attendance and profits? Or would it be wiser to have one or two seminars in a central area and have participants gather with reasonable travel comfort?
5. If you are having a meeting or conference where several seminars will be offered, be careful not to schedule them so that participants have difficulty deciding which one to attend. Unfortunately, if you give people the opportunity to choose between several seminars going on at the same time, several things can happen. They may attend one seminar for a period of time and then leave and go to another, hoping to pick up information from both or all of them. This is extremely disturbing to the speaker/trainer and to those attending. The other problem in offering concurrent seminars is that participants may not pay full attention to the seminar they are attending, but keep wondering what they are missing.

When selecting a date for a meeting with multiple seminars, consider adding a day or two for maximum results and benefits from all the seminars planned, rather than having concurrent sessions.

LOCAL EVENTS

Before selecting a seminar date, research the city and/or area in which you will be conducting your seminar. Are there conflicting events? You may be unfamiliar with these events if you live outside the seminar location. Annual festivals are an example. You would not want to book a seminar in Calgary, Canada, during the Fall Calgary Stampede. It is great fun, but hardly conducive to a learning experience.

If you are conducting a public seminar in a town or area that derives its income from one major industry or commercial endeavor, you could face an attendance problem. If there is an annual event such as a company picnic or Christmas party being held at the same time, this could have a disastrous effect on seminar attendance.

Another example of a local event may occur in an area that is predominately one ethnic or religious group. Check for holidays and special events. In many small towns the local high school or sporting events, homecoming parades, and/or charitable events are of major importance. You do not want to compete with these events.

On a broader scale are such things as the Mardi Gras in New Orleans, the Rose Festival in Portland, Oregon, the Renaissance Faire in the San Francisco Bay Area, and the Crosby Pro-Am Golf Tournament of the Monterey Bay Area in California. I'm sure you have the idea.

Contact the local chamber of commerce for this kind of information. They are most helpful and cooperative and will be able to assist you in selection of the most advantageous time to schedule your seminar.

STATE AND NATIONAL
HOLIDAYS AND EVENTS

Although state and national holidays are easier to recognize than local events, you will need to call the chamber of commerce or visitors and convention bureau in the seminar location. Ask which holidays allow for closure of banks, schools, or government offices. What special events are associated with these closures?

State holidays will vary. Not all states celebrate the same holidays, such as admission into the union.

Find out which events are not necessarily holidays (at the state or federal levels), but could affect seminar attendance—events such as election day, Super Bowl competition days, and the World Series. It is worth the extra time to do this additional research.

WEATHER CONDITIONS

Weather conditions should be strongly considered in the selection of seminar dates for the areas you wish to use. For example:

- Conducting a seminar in Hawaii during the rainy season may cause lengthy travel delays. The outer-island airports can be closed during bad storms.
- Going to Colorado, Utah, or Idaho for a winter seminar (with a little skiing on the side) sounds great, but consider closed airports, snow- and ice-clogged highways, and the accompanying difficulties.
- I participated in a seminar in New Orleans in July. It was an excellent seminar and the off-season rates were very attractive. However, there was a record-breaking heat wave all summer, and it was so hot and humid I could not leave the hotel. Even sitting by the hotel swimming pool was intolerable.
- Using the off-season for a seminar is a very good idea—just be sure you are prepared for the idiosyncrasies of the weather.

PARTICIPANTS' PERSONAL SITUATIONS

Last, but not least, in your date selection considerations are the personal situations of the participants. Here are some questions to ask yourself:

1. If you plan a seminar in June, will the age group of your participants be involved in graduation ceremonies?
2. Do their religious or ethnic backgrounds have events that could affect their willingness or ability to attend the seminar?
3. Conducting a seminar in an area where business is seasonal, you need to consider both sides of the situation:
    A. During the busy season can people take time off to attend?
    B. During the slack season, can they afford to attend?

Finally, in selecting the date or dates for your seminar, refer to a copy of *World Convention Dates* (see Section VI, Where Else Can I Get Help, for publication address). This publication will let you know who and what is in the same area you are using for your seminar. You will be better equipped to make a decision as to facility availability, transportation problems, and facility requirements for staging and logistics. You will be able to see who you will be competing with for services and facilities. You will be able to make a wiser choice of seminar dates.

If you have no choice of date or location and must conduct your seminar on a specific date at a specific location, you will at least be aware of the fact that it may be more difficult to plan and implement your seminar in a very popular and busy area and facility.

chapter eight
SPEAKER/TRAINER (S/T)

WHERE TO FIND
A SPEAKER/TRAINER

In the early stages of planning you have decided upon your seminar objectives. If you are in need of a speaker or trainer for your seminar, where will you find one? You will need a person or persons who will be able to fulfill your objectives in a manner and at a cost that is within your budget.

You may know someone you would like to have conduct the seminar. If, however, you have arrived at the time frame and the subject matter and have not chosen your S/T, you must now decide whom to use. You probably have an idea of the type of S/T and presentation style you want. Your budget could have a major effect on who you use as your S/T. You are now faced with a three-part question:

1. Who should you use as your S/T?
2. Will that person be able to present the material in the time frame you have available?
3. Will the cost of the S/T stay within your budget?

Hiring an outside S/T can be a very perplexing situation. Here are some suggestions to make your job easier.

HOW TO FIND
A SPEAKER/TRAINER

1. Ask other people in your profession, industry, or group whom they have used as an S/T. Were they happy with the results? What was the S/T fee schedule? Would they use the S/T again?
2. Research various directories from groups such as American Society of Association Executives, National Speakers' Association, Meeting Planners International, and American Society for Training and Development. The addresses and telephone numbers for these groups are listed in Section VI, Where Else Can I Get Help?
3. Consult the Yellow Pages for an S/T under the heading of Speakers' Bureaus.

STEPS TO TAKE WHEN YOU FIND
A PROSPECTIVE SPEAKER/TRAINER

1. When using a speakers' bureau to engage an S/T, ask all the questions listed in this section. Then ask the bureau to put you in direct contact with the S/T. You need to do this so that you can relate to them personally.

   Always reassure the bureau that you are not attempting to bypass them by dealing with the S/T directly. You simply need to communicate your specific needs to the S/T. Let them know that when you have made your decision about the speaker you will make the appropriate contractual arrangements with them.

   When you contact the speaker the bureau has suggested, ask as many questions as necessary to make your decision. It is customary and ethical to make all contractual and financial arrangements through the bureau, not directly with the S/T.
2. When working directly with an S/T, contact him or her as soon as possible. Many S/T's schedule months—and perhaps years—in advance.
3. Ask each prospective S/T as many questions as possible to make a confident, intelligent decision. Here are a few questions to start you on your way to that decision:
   A. How long have you been speaking/training?
   B. What are your credentials and background?
   C. Do you have a specific seminar to fit our needs? Can you design one for us or can you integrate your program and our material?
   D. Whom else have you worked for?
   E. May we call those past clients for recommendations and opinions of your work?

F. Do you have a promotional package you can send us?

G. Do you use audio or visual demonstration tapes? May we review them?

H. May we keep the demonstration tapes for our files, or should we return them?

I. May we attend a presentation you will be giving? If so, when and where?

J. With the outline of material and ideas described, can you conduct the seminar within our time frame?

K. Do you feel more than one S/T is required to make a successful presentation?

L. If the answer to question K is yes, who would you recommend?

M. What are your fees? Do you charge for preparation time?

N. If we were to use you for more than one seminar, do you have a multiple booking rate? If so, what is it?

O. If you will be using an S/T from another country, or if you will be conducting the seminar in a country other than your own, in what form will the fee be paid? U.S. funds net? German funds net, etc., check, money order, bank draft? Who will pay the foreign income taxes and when?

P. Do you provide a workbook or handout materials in your seminar? Can you send us a sample? Does your fee include these materials or do we provide them?

Q. Do you have materials such as books or cassette tapes that you offer to seminar participants? If so, what, and do these affect your fees?

R. Do you have a follow-up or postseminar program or communication vehicle? If so, what is it and is there a charge?

S. Do you have any other seminars in our area close to our date?

T. If the answer to question S is yes, do you prorate travel expenses?

U. What are your expenses and how do you cover them? Who pays for the travel, overnight accommodations, etc.? Do you provide an invoice? (Some S/T's include expenses in their fees, others do not.)

V. Do you require a retainer? If so, how much? When is it due?

W. If we choose you to be our S/T, how soon do you need to know?

X. Will you use our contract, or do you prefer to use your own?

4. After you have asked all of these questions of the various S/T's you are considering:

A. Review all of the answers and subsequent materials received. You may want to use a committee of your staff for this decision-making process.

B. Communicate with the past clients of the prospective S/T's and ask for opinions and recommendations.

C. Attend any S/T presentations possible.

D. If you cannot attend these presentations, review carefully the demonstration tapes. This is a very good alternative to actually attending a presentation.

E. After all the facts are collated, review how you *feel* about the various S/T's. Your confidence and rapport with them is second only in importance to their material and presentation.

If you follow these selection steps, you can be relatively confident that you have made a wise choice of your outside S/T.

If you are conducting the seminar yourself, the previous section obviously does not apply.

If you are using internal staff or someone from your group to conduct the seminar, here are some ideas to consider:

1. You will need to project the S/T costs in terms of preparation and presentation time, follow-up time, man-hours spent, and other related costs; e.g., will you need to have someone cover for the S/T while he or she is presenting the seminar?

2. Are you really sure the internal person or persons can do a good job? Have you actually been present at a seminar they have conducted?

3. Don't kid yourself about internal staff's ability to conduct the seminar. If using an outside S/T will be more effective, it may be worth the extra costs.

4. Don't take your internal S/T for granted. Provide them with all the appropriate materials you would give an outside S/T. Spend as much time on them and treat them just as you would an outside S/T.

CONTRACTS AND AGREEMENTS

As with any supplier you use for your seminar, you will need to have a contract or letter of agreement with your S/T. Be sure that the staff member in charge of the S/T sends any and all S/T communications to the planner's manual, while retaining copies for their own files, of course.

A contract or agreement can be as simple or as complicated as you find necessary. However, I always like to make life as simple as possible.

Here are the basic elements that should be included in the contract:

1. Your Company or Group Information:
   Name
   Address
   Telephone number
   Contact person(s)
2. Speaker/Trainer Information:
   Name, company name
   Address
   Telephone number
   Contact person(s), assistant, booking agent, etc.
3. Seminar Information:
   Location
   Address, telephone number
   Seminar title and specific facility room to be used
   General outline, if necessary
   Type of participants (general description of those attending)
   Number of participants
4. Speaker/Trainer Specifics:
   Audiovisual needs
   General description of handouts, workbooks
   Expense schedule and explanation (the handling of expenses should be carefully explained in this section):
   A. Who pays expenses? Do you reimburse the S/T for expenses incurred?
   B. Include in the expense arrangements items for air and ground transportation, overnight accommodations, food, and miscellaneous items such as tips.
   C. Who will make the travel arrangements for the S/T? You will save time, money, and perhaps embarrassment if these items are clearly explained and understood.
5. Retainer Information:
   If the S/T requires an advance retainer, this is the section where you make note. Include the date by which the retainer is due, to whom the payment is to be made, and what the final fees will be.
6. Invoice and Billing Information:
   If the S/T is to bill you for the services and you require an invoice, be sure to make note of this, as well as the date by which the invoice and billing are necessary.
   Many S/T's require payment at the conclusion of the seminar. If this is the case and you need lead time to have your accounting department issue a check, be sure to give yourself enough advance notice so you can obtain the necessary invoice.

7. Travel Arrangements:
    This section should have the complete travel arrangements for your S/T:
    A. Times of departure from his or her base and arrival at seminar location.
    B. Mode of transportation (airline, flight number), and ETA.
    C. How S/T is to travel to seminar facility from main source of transportation (cab, limo, picked up by you, etc.).

8. Overnight Arrangements:
    This is another area where you need to be very specific. The who, what, when, and where of your S/T's accommodations belong here. Who will be paying for the accommodations and how will the payment be made? In this section you should have a sentence that reads, "Upon arrival, S/T should contact the following person: _____ (Name the S/T contact person on your staff, and list their business and home telephone numbers and/or hotel room number.)

9. Recording Arrangements:
    If you have arrangements for recording the seminar, be sure to specify this and receive permission from the S/T to do so. Include information on what you will be doing with the recordings after the seminar.

10. Signatures and Dates:
    The last thing you need on the contract is a signature and date line for both you and the S/T.

As soon as you have made a firm commitment with your S/T, issue the contract. Have a copy for your planners' manual and a copy for the staff person in charge of communications with the S/T. Send two copies to the S/T. One is for his or her files and one is to be signed and returned to you.

CANCELLATIONS

There will come a time when the unthinkable happens!

Everything is going along just fine. Your seminar plans are humming right along, the participants are making arrangements to arrive, and your plans are coordinated for the seminar. All of a sudden the S/T must cancel.

Most S/T's I have known are very conscientious and would cancel only in the most dire emergency. But if it happens, you need to be prepared. In the beginning of your seminar plans, as you select your

S/T, acquire a list of three or four names of other S/T's who could be used in an emergency. Have their names, addresses, and telephone numbers in your planner's manual.

If your S/T finds it necessary to cancel, there are several things you need to do immediately:

1. Write a cancellation letter to the S/T. If there have been any retainer fees paid, request return of these within a certain number of days.
2. Make your S/T substitution choice and arrangements.
3. When your substitute S/T has been arranged, notify the participants of the change:
    A. If it is a public seminar you are presenting, and the people expect a certain S/T, you need to notify them as far in advance as possible. They should be given the option of cancelling their reservation to the seminar.
    B. If your seminar is in-house, you still need to notify the participants that there will be a change of seminar leaders. You don't want the participants to arrive and feel unhappy that the person they expected is not there, even if they have never seen or heard of him or her before. People draw all sorts of conclusions and have expectations based on the information received from you.

If for some reason it is necessary for *you* to cancel the seminar and you have arranged to have an outside S/T, you need to be prepared to pay a cancellation fee. Most S/T's book speaking dates far in advance and include cancellation-fee clauses in their contracts. Because of their busy schedules and the work done in preparation for your seminar, it is only fair that they be paid the full fee or a cancellation fee.

I hope that neither of these events occurs, and neither the S/T nor you must cancel. But if they do, your planning in advance with substitute S/T's will help overcome the problem. You'll sail smoothly over the rough seas to a happy and successful seminar.

PRESENTATION STYLE
AND ROOM SETUP

After you have decided upon your S/T and have gone through the various negotiations, discuss the presentation style to be used by the S/T. (In the section entitled Seminar Styles for Room Setup, I will cover the various styles and room setups you may wish to use.) Find out if the S/T has any specific audiovisual needs, and discuss the arrangements for lighting, stages, or risers, as well as all the other items needed for the seminar room.

Ask a Pro

Interview with:
Dr. Dru Scott
Author, HOW TO PUT MORE TIME IN YOUR LIFE and seminar speaker
San Francisco, California

SHEILA: What advice would you give to someone new to the job of staging seminars?

DRU: Learn from the best. Experience people who do well. Constantly put yourself in the position of being a customer.

When you attend different seminars you will start to appreciate all the things that go into making it a good learning experience. You will see that it is worthwhile caring for details such as not having to wait to register. You'll appreciate the fact that you have materials at hand, the fact that there's a "No Smoking" section, that the seats are comfortable and that they are far enough apart. You'll appreciate when the breaks are scheduled. That's what I call always maintaining a customer perspective. These things are easy to forget when you're on the other side.

SHEILA: Is there a single most important item in staging a seminar?

DRU: There are several items. First of all we hold our seminars in major luxury hotels. We have people greeting participants and paying special attention to them. Most people have a "don't be important" psychological injunction. Your seminar facility must say, "You are important."

When I first started doing seminars, the man I worked for said, "Don't believe what the hotels say, you go check it out." So we went to a hotel and checked things like the chairs, to be sure they're comfortable, how far the rest rooms are from the seminar room, where the air conditioning is and how to turn it on and off, how the lights work and where they are located. We checked everything.

SHEILA: In staging seminars, what do you think is the most common mistake?

DRU: I would say it is the lack of attention to details. Also, not maintaining customer perspective and not really understanding the makeup of your audience: their strengths, their needs, their wants.

SHEILA: Do you have a final comment?

DRU: Know the customer or the audience you're serving, really know them, not only in terms of age and occupation, but also their psychological needs and wants. What is most important to them? Understand them in terms of their time. Why are they at the seminar? If people are sent by their company to the seminar it is different than if they enrolled themselves. Understand your audience and understand your customers as a total entity.

SEMINAR BREAKS (TIME FRAMES)

Discuss the path of the seminar with the S/T. You may have a standard time for serving refreshments or food service. It could be in direct conflict with the S/T's presentation flow of materials and the dynamics of the group.

Your S/T should be closely consulted in these matters as you coordinate the facility plans. You want the serving of refreshments to be in harmony with the timing of the seminar itself. This point is often overlooked.

I attended a seminar where the S/T was building the group dynamics and we were all having an enjoyable time. We were working in dyads and triads. When we finished an exercise, the S/T announced that we would take a break for some beverages. We went into the hall area and found that the beverages had not arrived. The hotel had to be contacted and asked to bring them in. Of course, this took up a great deal of time, and the seminar was delayed. We lost some of our continuity and group dynamics.

SPEAKER/TRAINER PERSONAL NEEDS

There are a few extra items that would be appreciated if they are necessary:

1. Does the S/T need a queen- or king-sized bed?
2. Does the S/T need a bed board?
3. Is he or she a nonsmoker? Could you get nonsmoking accommodations?
4. Does the S/T have any special dietary needs?

These are all just commonsense things, but in the hustle and bustle of seminar managing they are often overlooked.

5. Changing Room: If you are using a large number of services provided by the facility, they can give you a complimentary "changing room," or at the very least, charge you a half-day rate. If the S/T does not need overnight accommodations, but will need a room to freshen up, this is a very thoughtful courtesy.

When discussing your S/T seminar style, there is a small but important item that is usually overlooked. That is the style of dress of the S/T and the seminar staff.

If the seminar is to have a relaxed, casual atmosphere, the S/T may want to dress in relaxed, casual attire. If it is important to maintain a highly professional image, a business-attire dress code would be more appropriate.

Dress code is one of the subtleties that can have a major effect on the participants. If the seminar is a very serious one with somewhat heavy material, it will have a less-than-serious appearance if the dress code is casual.

If the seminar includes discussing personal development or the personal lives of the participants, the S/T may wish to start out in a very businesslike attire, then take a jacket or tie off. This can change the mood to one that is more personal. It also encourages a more relaxed atmosphere among the participants.

The staff dress code will also play an important role in the overall effect. The same ideas apply for the seminar assistants and staff as for the S/T.

MISCELLANEOUS INFORMATION NEEDED BY THE S/T

There are a few items you need to provide your S/T so that he or she will be fully aware of what has preceded the seminar:

1. The S/T should have a full package of the seminar promotional materials and/or advertisements. This includes anything that you have used to promote the seminar, whether it is in-house or a public seminar. It is crucial that the S/T know what the participants have received. Their

expectations will be based on this information. There is often a lack of communication in this area, and it is very easy for a seminar to get off on the wrong foot because of this mistake.

2. Try to provide your S/T with as much information on the background of the participants as possible. If you are doing a preseminar questionnaire of a general nature, try to provide a compilation of the material on the various participants. If you are using a preseminar questionnaire for the S/T, he or she will, of course, have the necessary information for their presentation.

3. If you are having a conference or event of some kind where there will be more than one seminar, send each of your S/T's the name, address, telephone number, and basic outline of what the other S/T's will be presenting. It is very helpful to have your S/T's contact one another and share valuable information about the flow of material and ideas throughout the entire conference. It is a very fine way to make the S/T's comfortable about what is preceding or following their seminar.

4. Provide the S/T with a map or diagram of the facility when necessary. Include the names of a facility staff member and a member of your staff to contact if they need assistance before, during, or after the seminar.

5. Coordinate with the S/T the introduction he or she prefers.

SPEAKER/TRAINERS' MEETING

In the information to be sent to the S/T, set a time and location for a meeting where the S/T's can gather and share information. There are many things that can be accomplished in such a meeting. It is very helpful to be able to sit down with another S/T and go over the outline of material being presented. It is quite possible for one S/T to build a bridge to another S/T's seminar by mentioning the material to be presented or by referring to material already presented. In a large conference it can give the effect of a very close-knit S/T group, even though they all may have been strangers prior to this meeting.

Ask a Pro

Interview with:
Mr. Bill Bethel
Chairman of the Board, GETTING CONTROL, INC.
San Francisco, California

SHEILA: What advice would you give to someone new to the job of staging seminars?

BILL: The primary advice I would give anyone staging seminars, whether they are new or otherwise, is to begin the planning early. People believe that you can put on a seminar at a moment's notice. The truth is that there are a number of details to be handled that require lengths of time. Nothing happens as soon as you think it should. Give yourself as much time as possible.

SHEILA: Is there a single most important item in staging seminars?

BILL: I'd answer that by saying that there are many single most important items, depending from whose viewpoint you are seeing the seminar.

If you have plans for follow-through, then one of the most important items is the registration. Is it accurate and complete so that the list of attendees at various meetings will be available for the proper follow-through?

On the other hand, if you are the speaker, the setup of the room and the audio and visual equipment are the most important. All speakers want the room to fit their purpose. Some workshop leaders like round tables so the people have interplay with each other. Lecturers who are delivering material that requires notes may want the room set up classroom style. Speakers who are primarily motivational may use a ramp so they can get out into the audience.

If you are an individual who is responsible for a number of meetings at a convention, then the timing of each meeting and the flow from one meeting to another may be the most important item to you.

In general, a seminar is really an astounding number of details that must be coordinated to create the whole. It is very much like a piece of fine music. The individual notes have little meaning but, when orchestrated, make the beauty that stirs men's souls.

SHEILA: In staging seminars, what do you think is the most common mistake?

BILL: I think the most common mistake is the neglect of details. For example, are there tablecloths on the tables, water on the tables, ashtrays for smokers; has all equipment—audio and visual—been checked before the meeting, and a thousand other details.

The person who is in charge of putting on a seminar should be detail-oriented. That is what is required for success. From the beginning of the planning stage through the logistics of travel and lodging, to the hiring of speakers that fit the program most properly, to the actual meeting itself—a million details. The most common mistake is for the meeting to be painted with a broad brush instead of a fine one. The details are the most important.

SHEILA: Do you have a final comment?

BILL: Actually, the greatest speaker in the world, the plushest hotel, the finest resort will not make a successful meeting or seminar. They are all obviously contributory factors, but the big parts of a seminar that are easy to see do not come off unless the little things are attended to.

I guess the entire theme of my answers to these questions is that all of the parts are equally important, and no individual speaker or item can be the star in order to have a successful seminar.

chapter nine
SUPPLIERS

HOW TO SHOP FOR SUPPLIERS

As a consultant to individuals and companies, I have often heard these questions: How do I know which supplier, outside person, or company is qualified to do a good job and fill my needs? How do I know what is a fair price?

The answer is that you don't—unless you ask. People are often intimidated by the "expert syndrome." Just because people have titles after their name or they hang a sign on a door stating their business, that does not automatically make them experts. Nor does it mean they are qualified to handle your needs or problems.

Many local, state, and federal licensing agencies have certain training and skills requirements before a license is issued. However, even that does not mean the person is an expert or is qualified to help you.

It is your responsibility to your participants and to yourself to shop for the most qualified services and suppliers at the best possible price.

Don't be shy or intimidated. Ask as many questions as necessary to find out what you need to know. Constantly ask yourself, "Is this person or company *really* able to do the job for me?"

Here is a list of questions to help you get started. Develop your own questions for your special needs and add them to the list.

49

SHOPPING LIST QUESTIONNAIRE

1. What are the people's backgrounds in their field of specialization?
    A. What degrees and/or certifications or licenses have they received? (Does their service require any of these three?)
    B. What type and length of training did they receive?
    C. From whom and when did they receive these degrees, certifications, or licenses?
    D. If they are required by a licensing agency to have continuing education units, have they acquired them? What were they?
2. How long have they been in business?
3. Discuss their experience: e.g., has the travel agent been to, or had personal experience with, the locality of your seminar?
4. How many people do they have working for them? Is their staff large enough and do they have enough time to fulfill your needs?
5. Who else have they worked with on a project such as yours?
6. Do they have a reference list available? Are they willing to have you call their clients for opinions and references? (Take the time to call these people and inquire as to their satisfaction with this supplier.)
7. What is the price breakdown and range of their supplies or services?
8. Can they provide backup services and people if the primary arrangements go astray?
9. Have them specify, in writing, exactly what services they will provide for you (noting start and finish dates from your flow chart).
10. Arrange for specific follow-up dates (and then, of course, follow up) on both your part and theirs.

Go to several different people or companies with your list of questions and then compare the answers. Your decision will then be made upon well-researched facts.

However, a final suggestion on the subject of shopping for suppliers. Although you need as much expertise, experience, knowledge, and skill as possible, you also need to work in harmony with a person or company.

Try to find a balance between a person or company that can fulfill your needs and one that suits your personality. Sometimes, in the middle of a problem, good rapport can accomplish more than money or position power.

If a person lacks vast experience but is willing to work hard and find answers and solutions to your problems, and you have clear communications and good rapport, that may be a desirable combination.

Conversely, if your needs are so specialized that the choice of suppliers is limited, try for a harmonious relationship, but primarily look for the get-it-done-well person or company.

No matter what kind of supplier you are dealing with, the more links in the chain (people or things), the better chance of error. Don't take anything for granted. Stay in very close touch with your suppliers. Be diplomatic, but gently probe as to the progress of your project.

Another warning. Be very sure that the sales department and the production department are in agreement on such things as price, availability of their product or service, and delivery date. Many a seminar planner has a few more gray hairs over discrepancies or lack of communication between the sales department and the production department of suppliers.

When you have decided upon a supplier, share your flow chart and checklist with him or her. Help this person understand your needs and priorities.

As soon as the services or products have been discussed and initial steps agreed upon, write a letter of agreement or contract. If the services or products are especially intricate or costly, you may need to consult an attorney who specializes in such contracts.

LETTER OF AGREEMENT

Generally, a letter of agreement signed by all parties will suffice. Here are the things to include in your letter of agreement:

- Date: As soon as possible in your initial dealings with the supplier.
- From: Your name, address, title, telephone number, and any other information the supplier needs.
- To: Supplier's name, address, telephone number, any specific department name, and any other information you will need.
- Re: Invoice or purchase-order number or general description of product or service being ordered.

- Product/service description: Write a detailed and complete description of the product or service you are ordering. Changes can be made later when necessary.

- Cost breakdown/estimates: Describe in detail the complete costs or estimates as you understand them. Changes can be made later when necessary.

- Departments involved: Put the names of the departments and those responsible for these departments. If they are in different parts of a building or in a different physical location, include building numbers, addresses, telephone numbers, and any special information that is necessary.

- Delivery or shipping arrangements: State special and/or specific instructions as completely as possible when required.

- Financial arrangements: Deposits and payments along the way and final payments should be described completely. Distribution of payments to other suppliers working in conjunction with the specific supplier should also be completely described, e.g., payment to a typesetter working with a printer. Discounts, when applicable, should also be described. For example, you may receive a discount for a certain number or amount of items ordered, or discounts may be given in anticipation of future business.

  Be very precise and detailed in discussing any and all charges and/or fees.

- Starting, intermediate, and finishing dates: Outline any chain of events and dates that you anticipate for the completion of your order. From beginning to the final anticipated delivery date, leave nothing out.

- Special instructions or comments: This is your catchall category. Anything that does not fit in the other areas or needs should be stipulated here.

- Signature lines:

  Your name _____

  Your title _____

  Date _____

- Supplier:

  Supplier name _____

  Supplier title _____

  Date _____

Send two copies of the agreement, both signed by you, and ask for one copy to be returned to you with the supplier signature.

If you or the supplier make any changes after your original contract, write and sign and exchange an amendment to the initial agreement. It should contain:

> Reference to the original agreement date.
> Date of the change.
> The changes outlined (all changes should be outlined in complete detail just as in your original agreement).
>
> After changes have been described, put "All other parts of the agreement dated (date of original contract) _____ remain the same."
>
> Use the same procedure for signatures in the exchanging of this amendment as you did with the original contract.

If you use several suppliers, have one of your staff act as trouble-shooter. This person can work with your various staff members involved with other suppliers for their responsibilities to the seminar.

Remember, all communications—written or oral—should be noted and put in the file for that section of the seminar, then noted and sent to the planner's manual.

As with every other section, you should make use of a checklist and flow chart when dealing with suppliers.

From time to time, as your plan progresses, recheck your flow chart and checklist to make certain that you are on schedule. In closing this chapter on suppliers, I would like to say that the attitude of your suppliers toward you and your needs is very important. However, your attitude toward them is equally important. People will respond to you much quicker if you approach them with a basic trust and enthusiasm for their talents and abilities. Once you have decided upon a supplier, be as diplomatic and flexible as possible to insure a happy relationship. If you are called upon to solve an emergency or problem involving them, a soft, firm approach will get you a lot further than heated angry discussions. In all the years I have been involved in conducting and implementing seminars, it has been a rare exception when a supplier was not interested in doing a good job.

Ask a Pro

Interview with:
Mr. Jerry Richardson
President, RICHARDSON ASSOCIATES
San Francisco, California

SHEILA: What advice would you give to someone new to the job of staging seminars?
JERRY: Get advice from someone who knows the business.
SHEILA: Is there a single most important item in staging a seminar?
JERRY: Devise and implement a follow-up system to recheck/reconfirm all details and arrangements.
SHEILA: In staging seminars, what do you think is the most common mistake?
JERRY: Assuming that the hotel and catering people will do their jobs. You need to follow up with them continually.
SHEILA: Do you have a final comment?
JERRY: Attend to the details—or find someone who will!

Ask a Pro

Interview with:
Mr. LuVain G. "Boo" Bue
President, L.G. BUE & ASSOCIATES, INC.
Los Altos, California

SHEILA: What advice would you give to someone new to the job of staging seminars?
"BOO": After you have given the facility (hotel, etcetera) a complete, *written* diagram of how you want things set up, timing, etcetera, go over the plan with them in person several times. Then be prepared to adjust when they don't do what you expected them to do.
SHEILA: Is there a single most important item in staging seminars?
"BOO": Making sure the hotel *really* understands your needs, requirements, etcetera.
SHEILA: In staging seminars, what do you think is the most common mistake?
"BOO": 1) Assuming the facility (hotel, etcetera) will follow your instructions regarding setup, timing, and so on.
2) Not having knowledgeable help available (for registration, book/tape sales, etcetera).
SHEILA: Do you have a final comment?
"BOO": Congratulations to you for developing such a book!

54

chapter ten
AUDIOVISUAL (AV)

Your audiovisual requirements will be affected by budget, speaker/ trainer needs, seminar-room setup style, seminar site selection, and the number of seminar participants.

Before discussing the types of audiovisual equipment and their uses, let's examine their relationship to the factors listed above.

AN OVERVIEW

Budget

As a part of your budget, you need to consider the scope and sophistication of the equipment you wish to use. The best way to determine the audiovisual expenditure is to acquire a current catalog from a supplier. Contact several suppliers and have them mail you a catalog with the fullest range of products, equipment, and brands available. As you look through the catalogs, you may discover all sorts of clever and wonderful equipment that you didn't even know existed! As you review the equipment available, be aware of the price ranges. Is the equipment you need for rent, or must you buy it? This could make a big difference in

55

what equipment you finally decide to use. It also is a serious budgetary consideration.

Site Selection

As you conduct your on-site tour of the various seminar facilities, take your audiovisual checklist along. You can determine what equipment they have available, or what may need to be rented (either by you or the facility). You will have your comparison costs and prices with you, which will be helpful in comparing the facilities' audiovisual cost.

Some facilities will afford you more options. For example, a conference center will probably have more equipment on hand than a hotel. Depending upon your audiovisual needs, the type of site, (e.g., conference center versus hotel) may play a major role in budgetary considerations in site selection.

When you have ascertained what equipment will have to be rented, make sure there is a supplier near the facility that can fill your needs. Rarely do you want to become involved in shipping rented equipment. The liability is far too high.

Participants and Setup Style

The number of participants and the room setup style you use will also affect the audiovisual equipment needed.

If you are having a group of twenty people in the seminar, the size of a viewing screen can be smaller than if there are two hundred people. The need for sound equipment and such things as risers or tables to put viewing screens upon is also affected by the size of the group.

Your seminar-room setup style will dictate the same kinds of needs, plus such things as lengths of extension cords, etc.

There is a whole world of exciting audiovisual equipment, uses, training classes, associations, and information sources available.

Just as surely as I'm sitting here writing this section, there is some bright, creative person somewhere inventing, improving, or refining an important piece of audiovisual equipment. With this general information in mind, I now give *you* the responsibility to research the *best equipment* for your seminar for the *best possible price*.

AUDIO EQUIPMENT

Audio Recording Equipment

If you plan to record all or part of a seminar, the future use and purpose of the recording is important. In recording the seminar to study and improve the material (and/or the presentation), a simple cassette recorder would probably be fine. You could leave it on a table and have someone change the tapes. You could plug it into the house system and the sound will be quite acceptable. Something as small as micro-mini cassette portable dictating equipment could be used; or you could use something as large as the professional cassette recorders.

If the recording will be used for producing reproductions of the material from the seminar, you have many choices of equipment. There are many fine cassette recorders that produce excellent quality tapes. These can be transferred to a reel-to-reel system for editing and reproduction from a master copy, called a running master. You could also go directly to a reel-to-reel system during the seminar. These are usually plugged into the house public-address system. Then the editing can be done in a one-step rather than a two-step process. Unless someone in your group is familiar with reel-to-reel equipment, it may be necessary to hire a professional to do the recording.

Another option is to take the cassette tapes and reproduce directly from the cassette tape on a high-speed reproducer. This equipment is available and should be researched if you are planning on reproducing the tapes either for group study or sales.

Microphones

Of all the material in this book, there is no subject that comes close to the intensity of emotion I have about microphones and the accompanying sound system. This is a hot button. As a speaker/trainer, I have worked in rooms that were poorly lit, badly staged, and set wrong. These can be overcome more easily than a bad microphone and/or poor sound system. Be very, very careful when it comes to filling your speaker/trainer needs in this area. Do not allow *any* facility to tell you they will take care of the matter and you need not worry. Check, doublecheck, and check again. Be sure that the system works and is exactly what you need and want. If you don't know what you need or want, do a thorough research job on the types of microphones and sound systems available. During your on-site tour, ask the facility staff person to let you hear and try out their system. There are many types of microphones available.

A FIXED LECTERN MICROPHONE is attached and must be spoken into at a relatively close range. This is very poor for a seminar of any length. The speaker/trainer is restricted to one spot. Some of these lecterns have the sound system built into them, others are plugged into a house public-address system.

A HAND-HELD MICROPHONE gives variety of movement. It can be placed in a stand, which can be attached to a lectern or can be free-standing (the shorter version sits on a table; the taller version is one that stands several feet high and can be adjusted to various heights). There are many sizes and shapes of hand-held microphones. Personally, I do not care to use hand-held microphones. For a seminar they are a nuisance. It is difficult to write on a blackboard, hold notes, and try to hold a microphone too. It can also be very tiring to hold a microphone all day long. I prefer a lavaliere, clip-on, or wireless microphone.

A LAVALIERE MICROPHONE has an attachment (usually a cord) that goes around the speaker/trainer's neck and connects to the micro-phone. This arrangement put the microphone at approximately collar-bone height on the chest. It is less distracting than a hand-held micro-phone and is relatively easy to put on and take off.

A CLIP-ON MICROPHONE has an attachment similar to a tie tack or tie clip, into which the microphone fits. This is then attached to the speaker/trainer's clothing at mid-chest location. When the tie tack or tie clasp fits well and doesn't jiggle or drop the microphone, this is a very comfortable microphone to use. It is usually easy to put on and take off, and can be adjusted easily on the clothing. When using a lavaliere, clip-on, or hand-held microphone, you can arrange to have an exten-sion cord attached to give your S/T maximum mobility.

WIRELESS MICROPHONES are great when they work and are used in a room that doesn't interfere with their signal to the amplifier. Wireless microphones are sometimes prone to interference from radio stations or citizens' band radios (CB's) in the area. If you are in a room that has steel construction, it can block transmission to the amplifier.

There are still some kinks to be worked out in wireless microphones, but when they work well they are a dream. It is worth the effort to explore the possibility of using a wireless microphone.

Regardless of which type of microphone you decide to use, there is one cardinal rule—*always* have a backup microphone, live and ready to use. It should be placed in the front of the room with the speaker/trainer, at a position that is easy to pick up immediately if the primary microphone malfunctions. The added expense of a secondary microphone is far outweighed by the advantages if and when it is needed.

You may be interested in exploring the purchase of a microphone, rather than renting one or using what is available at the facility. If you purchase your own microphone you will need a full range of adapters to take to the facility. You cannot guarantee that your microphone plug will fit into the house public-address system, thus the need for a choice of adapters.

VISUAL EQUIPMENT

A successful seminar usually includes some sort of visual aid. Since a major part of our perception is visual, the equipment you choose and use should be well tailored to your presentation style and the material being presented.

The advantage for the participants is that they receive your information both visually and auditorially. The advantage for the speaker/trainer is that the visual aids can be used as an outline for the material being presented.

One thought to keep in mind is that any visual aid should be a backup of ideas and material, not the whole presentation. Any presentation that relies too heavily on visual aids is just as bad as one that uses none.

Let's take a look at the most popular types of visual aids available to you.

Film Strips

These are easy to transport and are adaptable for any size group. There are the portable sound film-strip projectors that have a built-in screen for rear and front projections. These portable console models are best used with small groups that can gather around the screen. The silent film-strip projectors can be used for larger groups, with the image projected onto a regular viewing screen placed in the front of the room. These models can also be used with a synchronized audio cassette player. It does take some expertise and expense to produce film strips; however, there are the write-on film strips that can be prepared by hand, with clever drawings, tracings, or appliqués. These give you some flexibility and variety in your presentation. A disadvantage of a film strip is that you cannot change the order in which you are using it, as you can with a slide presentation. Once you prepare the film, you must present it in that order.

A normal movie screen can be used for projection, and you need to carry a replacement lamp (bulb) with you.

Overhead Projectors

This type of projector is a very popular medium for visual aid in a presentation. It is easy to transport and can be used with any size group. The images are projected onto a movie screen appropriate for the size of your group. The expertise required to use the overhead projector can be as simple or complicated as you wish. Something as easy as a clear transparency that you write on with a marker pen as you make your presentation is certainly acceptable. A more complicated process might involve color transparencies, artwork, and on into sophisticated graphs and charts. Your expertise will develop as you use materials. There are kits with all of the materials and samples of the most widely used items for production of transparencies available at art and stationery stores. You can spend as little or as much as you choose. If you can afford to own your own overhead projector, this will, of course, entail an initial outlay of money. If you do not wish to purchase one, they are available for rental at a nominal fee. The equipment you need to have with you would be some clear acetates, your marker pen and pencils, and a replacement lamp (bulb).

Slide Projectors

The use of slides in your seminar can be quite interesting and a fine visual aid. One of the advantages of using slides, as opposed to a film strip, is that the slides can be put in different order, eliminated, or added to as you feel necessary, rather than being stuck with the predetermined order and presentation of a film strip. The problem involved in slides is that they can be lost or put in the wrong order more easily. Slides and slide projectors are easy to transport and can also be used with any size group. There is a console slide/sound projector similar to the film strip console. It is a unit with a screen for rear or front projection and is able to produce the sound portion right along with the picture. This type is easy to carry. However, they are limited to a smaller group. Some of them have the adaptability of projecting their image onto a screen, which makes them usable in any situation. There are, of course, the regular slide projectors with a carousel or slide tray to hold the slides. They can also be keyed with an audio cassette tape that you can use quite easily. The expertise required to use a slide projector and/or a sound/sync package is dependent upon the sophistication of your program. An audio tape can be easily keyed to the slides by using a script and carefully studying your slides. The preparation of the slides may be a more difficult project, depending upon how you prepare them. Some can be photographs, others can be prepared as the film strip was, with a write-on transparency that has been cut and prepared for the slide. The slide presentation may be more expensive if you want to own the equipment but it is also available for rental at a nominal fee.

Equipment that you need to have with you would be: a replacement lamp (bulb), extra slides, and perhaps an audio cassette tape duplicate. One disadvantage of a slide presentation is that the room must be darkened. This does not enable the participants to take notes as well as when you use an overhead projection.

Movie Projectors

The use of movies certainly has its place in seminar conducting. A disadvantage is the need for a darkened room, as with slides, which does not allow as much note taking as other media. However, the advantage of sight, sound, color, and motion gives the participants a very realistic experience, and the retention level of information is higher.

Movie projectors are easy to transport, as are most films. They are usable for any size group and the expertise needed to run a movie projector is minimal. If you choose to prepare your own films, it becomes a very expensive visual medium. However, there are many fine films that can be rented or purchased, cutting the expense. A problem that is involved with using movies is that you can't stop the film as easily, discuss a point, and then continue. So a great deal of work needs to be done by the seminar speaker/trainer in preparing materials to be used before or after the movie. When using a movie projector, be sure to have a take-up reel. Often times, rented projectors will not have this take-up reel and, of course, then you cannot show the film. The only replacement part needed for a projector is a lamp (bulb). If your budget allows, it is a very good idea to have two copies of the same film running simultaneously, one with sound and light turned off, so that if the main projector or film should malfunction, the second can be immediately turned on without a loss of continuity.

Video Equipment

This equipment is not easily transported. When you need to carry a camera, recorder, and monitor, it can be difficult. They may be rented or may be available at your facility site. The use of video equipment is very effective and is becoming more and more popular. The size of the group using the equipment depends upon the style of presentation, material, and expertise of the speaker/trainer. It does take a good deal of training to use this equipment properly; it should not be embarked upon lightly. It is also a very expensive medium, and the list of auxiliary equipment that you need is as long as the original list of equipment. As more and more courses develop and the cost of video equipment is reduced, this will increase in popularity as a visual-aid tool.

Lecterns

There are several variations on lectern styles. Your speaker/trainer will be able to tell you what kind, if any, he or she may need. Here are some styles available:

1. A plain lectern with no audiovisual equipment attached. It can be a full-length freestanding size, or a desk/table top, smaller version. If you

are using a tabletop lectern (one that is placed on a stand or table, not freestanding), be sure the table size fits your needs. Sometimes it is quite handy to have a table right next to the speaking area, on which to put material or other equipment. The speaker/trainer style and experience will indicate which is best. Lecterns come with a variety of internal parts. Some are nothing more than a collapsible shell with supports inside that can easily be moved about. Others are ponderous and take real strength to move. There is generally a shelf of some sort on which to put papers or a glass of water. Check to be sure that the shelf is secure. I forgot to do this once and put a cup of tea on the shelf the first thing in the morning— it collapsed! Everyone reacted as would be expected, and it was a very amiable group all day long—but I had one soaked leg and shoe.

Some lecterns have a drawer just under the top; sometimes, if it's an older model, it may have shelves behind doors.

Many speaker/trainers use a lectern simply to keep them company in the working area. Others have a lot of contact and use it with purpose. Whatever your speaker/trainer's style, be careful where you place it on the stage, riser, or floor. You may not be able to move it once you have set it up, and this might cause a problem during the seminar.

2. There are other kinds of lecterns with attachments to hold microphones and a small light.

3. There are those with all sorts of equipment and control panels for audiovisual presentations. These can be quite complicated and sophisticated.

If the speaker/trainer will be using the lectern microphone, test the sound to determine how close or how far a speaker can stand before voice distortion occurs.

Easels and Pads

If you need an easel and writing pad, your audiovisual supplier catalog will show you a range of choices. These are personal items on which every speaker/trainer has an opinion. If the speaker/trainer uses one, he or she will have a type in mind. But here are a few general points to remember:

1. Easels are not easy to transport. They also become damaged in a very short time, so the expense of buying one may be unnecessary. They can be rented.

2. The pads can be prepared partially or fully in advance of the seminar. You can use the kind with squares to guide lettering. These can be marked

with a light blue pencil (acting as a guide) and then done in dark ink during the seminar.

3. A flip chart could be used in place of an easel and pad. Be sure that the flip chart contains enough paper for your purpose.

4. When using either of these tools, be sure they are big enough and bright enough to be seen by all the participants. If they are not, consider using an overhead projector.

5. If you are going to use an easel, it is important to check its strength to insure that it will not collapse under the weight of the paper pad or when you are writing on it.

Bulletin Boards

Bulletin boards can be used quite effectively when graphics are attached. They are available in cork, fabric, and magnetic surfaces. They can be placed in front of the speaker/trainer working area, or on the side of the seminar room. During the seminar your graphics can be attached, creating a dynamic presentation style.

Chalkboards

Chalkboards range in sizes and colors. Again, check your audiovisual supplier catalog. There are visual-aid boards that act as chalkboards except that you write with marking pens rather than chalk.

The freestanding chalkboards are often reversible. However, they are not very portable. Sometimes these large chalkboards have wheels with locking devices. Be sure the locks work. It is pretty hard to chase a board around while you're trying to write on it and talk at the same time.

Do not allow well-meaning people to wash a chalkboard so that it looks nice and clean—*ouch!* That clean board will squeak and give your audience chills. Use a clean eraser and erase well.

Dustless chalk that comes in white or yellow is easiest on the hands and clothing. You can also purchase an aluminum chalk holder. You simply slip the chalk into it and use it like a pencil, turning it to release more chalk. That way you never have to touch the chalk directly.

Whenever you use any audiovisual equipment, have a supply of spare parts available at all times. Purchase or rent them, but don't leave home without them!

The more complicated the equipment, the more time you need to allow for testing everything to make sure it all works.

AUDIOVISUAL AND THE FACILITY

1. Check during your on-site tour whether the facility is required to use union people for the audiovisual presentations you need. Find out the hourly rates, how many union people are required, and for what functions.
2. Have someone from your staff or a facility staff member available during the seminar to assist all audiovisual presentations. If someone on your staff is trained in audiovisual, have the facility show and explain to them the hows and whys of the house systems and equipment.
3. Establish a close relationship with the facility audiovisual department. Keep them posted during your preseminar and advance-work stages. Let them know well in advance of any changes or additions needed.
4. Last but not least, arrive early and check, check, check the facility systems and all the audiovisual equipment you will be using.

Ask a Pro

Interview with:
Dr. Eden Ryl
President, RAMIC PRODUCTIONS
Newport Beach, California

SHEILA: What advice would you give to someone new to the job of staging seminars?

EDEN: Constantly question what you are trying to achieve. When people come together in a meeting it is usually for the purpose of communication of some sort. And in staging a session, if every decision you make and every detail that you cover is based on this premise, you will probably be on target.

Some hotels and catering departments are well managed and the setting up will go very smoothly. But don't take this for granted. Anticipate possible mistakes and then try to avoid them in advance by making your desires easy for the staff to understand. Prepare a facility list and include a diagram of what is needed. Then the staff can both see and read what you want.

Indicate on the diagram the risers (height needed), where the lectern should be placed (at the side of the stage, the middle, or where?), chairs, tables, a movie screen. Draw in the positions. Anything that you want on stage should be indicated on the drawing.

Also indicate the position of chairs in the auditorium. You will probably want them staggered for better visibility. Even tell the setup people how many chairs should be in a row. If left on their own, sometimes they put chairs so far off to the side that viewing is difficult. Remember, you want to be sure communication is taking place.

The written/visual instructions should be given to the catering sales department several days before the meeting. And then on the actual day of the meeting, be on hand while setting up is going on to be sure that your desires are carried out.

Be sure the room is set up in plenty of time so that you can check out details before the first participants arrive. Check the mike, check the focus on the projector. It gives you time to be sure the chairs are properly placed. Many times I've had to move chairs myself because the setup people disappeared, never to be seen again.

It's astonishing how carelessness can wreck a meeting—failure to be sure of no ringing phones in the room, or forgetting to instruct the catering department that serving must be finished and all service people must be out of the room when the speaker begins—no clearing of dishes, or not checking the mike ahead to be certain there are no loose wires. What may seem like obvious details may, when overlooked, become barriers between the speaker and the audience.

SHEILA: Is there a single most important item in staging a seminar?

EDEN: It's difficult, Sheila, to narrow the order of importance down to one item. Myriad details go into a successful meeting. However, it seems that one of the most overlooked items is certainly lighting. The general illumination in the room itself is seldom enough. The speaker needs to be easily visible. Spotlights are too hot and much too uncomfortable from the speaker's standpoint. Floodlights give the same effect without the heat.

Being able to see the speaker's facial expressions, mannerisms, use of arms and body all make it easier for the audience to listen and to enjoy and comprehend the message.

Lighting the speaker is not enough. The individual should also be on a stage, riser, or platform high enough so that everyone has a clear view of what is going on. Anything you can do to make the group feel comfortable will insure a more appreciative audience.

SHEILA: In staging seminars, what do you think is the most common mistake?

EDEN: As you know, Sheila, television plays a dominant role in the lives of many people, so audiences today are visually oriented. Therefore, more and more program and seminar leaders are including films in their meetings.

Very often the seminar coordinator will call an equipment rental company and ask for a 16mm projector and screen to be at the meeting room by a certain time, and then they think that's the end of it. But it is wise to be specific. Ask for a fast-fold screen (an absolute must if the meeting is over 150 people) and give the exact size needed. (Again, this is dependent upon the size of the group. A larger picture is, of course, usually more impressive.)

Also indicate to the rental firm if you need an automatic load, an extension cord, or perhaps an additional speaker.

When the equipment arrives—well in advance of the meeting time—be sure to check the projector. Be sure that it is clean and lint-free. Is there an extra bulb? Does the projector itself run quietly or is it so old that it is much too noisy? Is the picture sound steady? Thread it up and try it before the delivery person leaves.

If at all possible, plug into the hotel sound system so that everyone can hear without difficulty.

Two projectors running at the same time, one with the light off as a backup, is a good idea. It means, of course, that you must have two prints of the film and start them at the same time. Then if something happens to the projector during the screening you can switch to the other machine without losing time or continuity.

Be sure that the picture is projected using every bit of space at the top of the screen, so that your audience can view the picture without interference.

Showing a motion picture adds a lot of pizzazz to a conference, and it is worth taking the time to be sure that the equipment is in good working order.

SHEILA: Do you have a final comment?

EDEN: Check out the details and be sure that *anything* that affects the enjoyment of the audience and the enhancement of the communication process is taken care of. Then people will know that you care and will recognize you as a professional.

It's up to you.

chapter eleven
SEMINAR ROOM SETUP STYLES

The objectives and goals of the seminar have been outlined, so you know the approximate length of the seminar (one-half day, one day, three days, or whatever). You also know if you will need overnight accommodations. You know approximately how many participants will be in attendance. Your budgeting outline has been set. You have decided who you plan to use as your seminar S/T; their presentation style and possible room setup have been discussed. You also know the audiovisual requirements, which you have outlined with your S/T.

Before you can make a seminar facility selection and go on to arranging travel, you need to make a general decision as to the style of seminar room setup you wish to use. When this is done you can more easily consider the various types of facilities available for your seminar.

This may be a quick, easy process for you. For example, if you wish to conduct a seminar as part of a cruise ship vacation, your facility selections will be narrowed to the types of ships available rather than the various land facility choices. In this case, you will probably have to take what you can get for a room setup style.

If, however, your choice is not as narrow as that, you need to consider the room setup styles most commonly used.

With this information in hand, you will be able to decide easily which facilities you wish to inspect and can eventually choose one for your seminar location.

The seven most commonly used styles of room setup are: amphitheater, classroom, banquet, theater, U shapes, chairs only, and floor/ground sitting. Each style has pluses and minuses. Let's examine each one individually.

STYLE NUMBER ONE
AMPHITHEATER

This style will be in either a theatrical or an educational facility. In both these types of facilities the participants will have a clear view of the front area where the S/T will be standing. You will know exactly how many people the room holds. You can use ushers to fill the seating (people are used to being ushered in this type of setting).

There is less resistance to filling the front rows, and the acoustics are sometimes designed to carry voices with little or no amplification. There will probably be a projection booth or area available for audiovisual equipment.

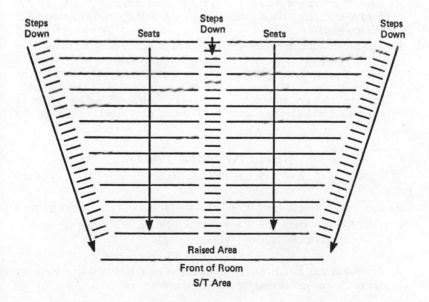

If you use a theater and wish to present a dramatic effect or a performance-type presentation, this is the ideal place to do it. However, there is no writing surface available for the participants, which can cause a problem if your seminar runs more than one hour in length.

If you use an educational facility that is amphitheater style, you will evoke the structured, classic educational responses from the participants.

Some of the negative points with either of these two room styles are:

1. You are stuck with fixed seating (no flexibility).
2. Unless you fill all the seats, there will be a feeling of emptiness (even if you block off the part of the seats that you don't want used).
3. In a theater, people expect to be entertained rather than to participate or be open to a learning process.
4. In an educational amphitheater, you will evoke the classroom response in people. As I mentioned in the types of facilities available, you may or may not like the results, depending upon the participants' personal experience while they were in school.
5. In a theater, people sitting in the front rows must bend their necks to look up to the stage (hard to do for a long time). In an educational facility where the front of the room is at the bottom of the amphitheater, it is hard to maintain a close, intimate feeling with the participants sitting in the top rows.
6. The S/T conducting your seminar needs to be experienced in working with these types of setup. If he or she is not, it could cause a problem in terms of presentation styles. If the S/T is accustomed to standing directly on the floor at the same level as the participants and all of a sudden he or she must be up on the stage or down at the bottom of the seating, he or she may not be able to maintain eye contact or rapport.

STYLE NUMBER TWO
CLASSROOM

Classroom style refers to seating that has tables and chairs set in rows facing the front, where the S/T will be working.

The pluses of classroom style setup are:

1. Practically any facility can set a room this way. If they do not have the tables (or enough tables) they can easily rent them.

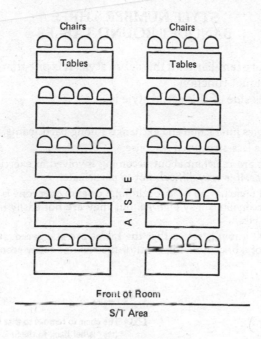

Chairs · Chairs

Tables · Tables

A I S L E

Front of Room

S/T Area

2. The setup is relatively quick. A room diagram in this style is familiar to most setup crews.
3. A room at almost any facility will seat more people classroom style than in banquet rounds (but less than theater style).
4. Obviously, the participants have a comfortable writing surface; also, a cup of coffee or a glass of water is easily accommodated.

The minuses of classroom setup are:

1. It also elicits a more "classroom" type of response. Do you want this? If so, good; if not, beware!
2. If the participants are to interact in dyads or triads, etc., they will be stuck with the people they are sitting next to. It is not easy to turn around and interact with other people in this setup style. Depending upon the size of the room and number of participants, this style can be difficult to fill or empty quickly.
3. If you have a small number of people, using this style can create an empty feeling in the room, as opposed to a U shape or round tables.

71

STYLE NUMBER THREE
BANQUET ROUND TABLES

Most people are familiar with this setup style. It is one that we find at a dinner or banquet function.

The plus side of this setup style is:

1. It promotes interaction and exchange among participants.
2. It elicits a less-structured response.
3. If people are reluctant about becoming involved in exercises or verbal exchanges, it is very difficult not to participate.
4. A round table has no head, beginning, or end; everyone is equal (dominant personalities may emerge, but they are not easily maintained at round tables).
5. When the room is set so that the tables are staggered, such as in the pattern of a brick wall, the front of the room is easily seen.

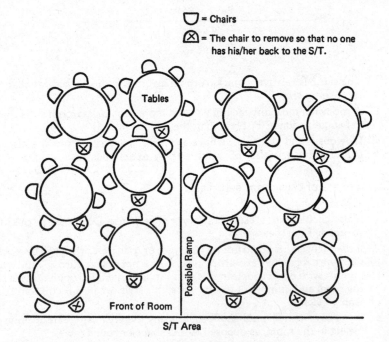

= Chairs

= The chair to remove so that no one has his/her back to the S/T.

Tables

Possible Ramp

Front of Room

S/T Area

72

The minuses of banquet style setup are:

1. Round tables in a room do not accommodate as many people as theater or classroom style.
2. Not all facilities have round tables and linens for the tables. They are not always readily available for rental.
3. People are hesitant about using round tables because they feel that someone at the table will always have his or her back to the S/T. That is easily solved. If the table holds six around, simply remove the sixth chair that would have its back to the S/T (the same goes with eight or ten around). The other five chairs can be placed around the table so they face the S/T. If the participants simply take notes and do not interact, they sit as the chairs are placed. If you want them to interact, they will turn their chairs and do so. It works quite well.

   Some S/T's are afraid that all the turning back and forth will cause distraction. That is true to an extent, but the feeling of involvement that the participants have outweighs the problem.

STYLE NUMBER FOUR
THEATER STYLE

The term *theater style* means that the seating is chairs only, which are placed in rows, like a theater. The major thrust of this setup is that it always allows maximum seating in any particular room. Unfortunately, there are more minuses than pluses to this setup:

1. The participants have no writing surface other than what they can carry and use in their laps.

Chairs Only   Chairs Only

AISLE

Front of Room

S/T Area

2. There is little possibility for interaction.
3. For a true seminar, participants will feel boxed-in if they must sit for any length of time.
4. A clear view of the front is difficult. You must always use risers in this setup if there are over forty participants.

STYLE NUMBER FIVE
TABLES IN U SHAPE

Rectangular tables with chairs set around and one end empty makes a very nice seminar setup. Place them in a U shape, as shown in the diagram. The S/T can move within the U shape or can work at the front of the room, as well. This setup gives a feeling of close contact and intimacy. It is great for interaction. Another advantage is if the room you are using is oddly or badly shaped, you can create your own shape without depending upon a standard classroom or theater style.

The diagram shows eight tables, with seven chairs at each table. You can use smaller or larger U shapes, depending upon your needs.

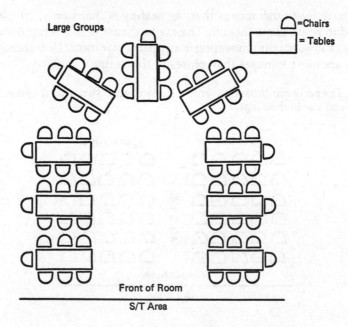

Large Groups

◯ =Chairs

▭ = Tables

Front of Room

S/T Area

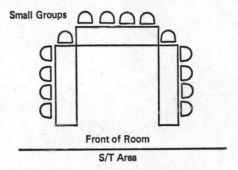

Small Groups

Front of Room

S/T Area

The only minus is that you obviously can't use this style if you are having a large number of participants (seventy-five or more). The diagram above shows a modified version of this setup.

You will notice that it has the same effect and appeal as the diagram on page 74, but it is for fewer people. You might use this when the group is small and the classroom or theater styles or round tables will give a feeling of emptiness in a room that is extra large.

There can be one or several tables in either the sides or the top of this formation. If you have a few extra participants, they could be seated on the inside of the U as well. This is not best, but could do in a pinch.

Using either of these U-shaped styles will definitely require a diagram for the facility setup crew. They will never understand what you want by verbal description or explanation alone.

STYLE NUMBER SIX
CHAIRS ONLY

If your seminar style is more relaxed, with more interaction among the participants, using chairs only gives an interesting style. It is impossible for participants to sit in a circle and not take part. One of the minuses is lack of writing surface (unless you are at an educational facility and have chairs with writing surfaces attached). Again, as in theater style, you can't sit very long and effectively take notes with chairs only. Chairs, however, can be used very effectively when moved into sub-

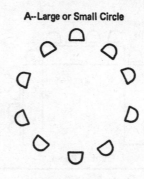

A--Large or Small Circle

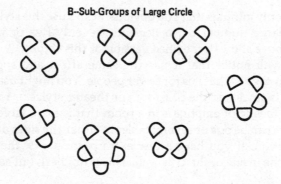

B--Sub-Groups of Large Circle

groups. It is a setup style that can be used in any facility other than one with fixed seating attached to the floor.

A chairs-only setup is best used in smaller groups. So if your group size is forty or more, this style will not work very well.

STYLE NUMBER SEVEN
FLOOR/GROUND SITTING

Floor sitting is not a setup to be used for an extended period of time. It is an interesting break from the norm and can be adapted as a *part* of a seminar. Using almost any of the other major setup styles, subgroups can be created with floor or ground sitting. If you are at a facility that has the space to allow you a regular setup and this subgroup style, you may want to actually use another room for this, or split a large room with dividers and use half for the regular setup and half for the floor sitting. The physical action of leaving a regular setup to sit on the floor will give you a very interesting change of pace. It will also be a psychical break which you may use to your advantage.

Floor sitting is also a great equalizer. Dominant personalities tend to be less so, and people all tend to relax more and open up more while seated on the floor.

I remember once I was conducting a seminar with twenty-five participants at a junior college. The structure and dominant classroom effect was blocking communications between participants, so I adjourned to the lawn area just outside of the building, and we all sat on the ground. It was amazing to see the difference in openness and attitude of the participants.

If you plan to sit on the floor or ground, arrange to have some sort of mat or pad available for comfort and cleanliness. It is also a good idea to inform the participants in advance that there will be floor sitting and to dress accordingly.

In closing this section on seminar room setup styles, I want to point out that there is no "best" or "right" way.

Your seminar material, S/T style, participants' background, and physical facility location will dictate the style to use.

Just don't be afraid to try a new or different style than you are accustomed to.

Always present an exact diagram to the facility of the style you wish to use. Don't assume that they will understand.

Ask a Pro

Interview with:
Mr. Terrence J. McCann
Executive Director, TOASTMASTERS INTERNATIONAL
Santa Ana, California

SHEILA: What advice would you give to someone new to the job of staging seminars?

TERRENCE: There are several things. First, it's vitally important that a meeting planner understands the needs, wants, and goals of the seminar participants. He or she must then find the right speaker who has the knowledge and experience and the material that will help meet those needs and goals.

It's vital that the meeting planner balance the seminar so that there is the right amount of lecture versus participation on the part of the audience. We have a common formula that there should be some type of participation or involvement every fifteen or thirty minutes into a seminar session.

It's important that the meeting planner select the right room and conference site surroundings. For example, you would probably put top executives into a comfortable resort where the atmosphere meets with their particular life-styles as well as their wants. The room itself, the size, ceiling height, amount of light, and access to out-of-doors all have a bearing on the success of the meeting.

SHEILA: Is there a single most important item in staging a seminar?

TERRENCE: If I were to give the three most important items in staging a seminar, they would be:

1. Pay attention to timing; always start sessions on time and end on time.
2. Speaker selection. Find the best possible person to meet the needs of the audience.
3. The meeting settings, the rooms, and the total environment must be right for the total audience.

SHEILA: In staging seminars, what do you think is the most common mistake?

TERRENCE: I've been around associations and organizations that are so careful about these things that I haven't observed too many mistakes. But if you ask the speakers, they will tell you the planner who fails to assign someone to make certain that every one of the speaker's needs is being met is neglecting an important part of his job. I'm talking about everything from promotion to taking care of rooms for the speaker, getting him or her properly introduced and sending a thank-you note afterwards. If all the fine details are not being met by a specialist working with the speaker, then the meeting planner is making a mistake.

SHEILA: Do you have a final comment?

TERRENCE: I spent five years planning, developing, coordinating, and even conducting seminars for the Supermarket Institute in Chicago, a leading food educational association. We were very, very thorough in making certain that our speakers had the right chemistry. That's vital. The meeting planner must make sure the speaker is talking on the right subject, that his or her style is compatible so he or she will have the right impact. There's a lot of work involved there. For example, you've got to interview the speaker thoroughly before he or she comes into your meeting. You've got to make certain that the speaker's introduction is as good as the speech. That's one thing we insist on at our Toastmasters International Convention. The introduction has to be as good as the speech so the audience is warmed up and ready to receive the speaker.

chapter twelve
TRAVEL ARRANGEMENTS

Our society is so mobile that the majority of people have had some sort of travel experience. Try not to get involved in making travel arrangements for your seminar participants. They can probably handle it themselves. But if you must handle their arrangements, or want to do so, have one staff person in charge. It will save confusion, time, and errors.

If the participants are making their own arrangements, it is highly professional and courteous on your part to provide them with helpful information. Your thoughtfulness and consideration for their travel needs will be greatly appreciated.

Regardless of who is handling the travel arrangements, here are some tips to make the job easier.

CHAMBERS OF COMMERCE AND/OR VISITORS' AND CONVENTION BUREAUS

Contact one or more of these groups at the location of your seminar. Discuss with them your travel needs and ask for any suggestions or help they might be able to give. I have found these two groups to be very helpful. Some of the information they have provided I would never have found in other places or from other sources.

YOU AND YOUR STAFF

Don't forget that the same arrangements and requirements for the participants' travel apply to you and your staff. Assign someone the task of taking care of these internal travel details. You and your staff may wish to arrive earlier and stay later than the seminar participants. Be sure you make specific arrangements if overnight accommodations are necessary. If your staff comprises a large enough group you may qualify for a charter or group rate in both travel and overnight accommodations. Sometimes a certain number of days, or traveling over a certain time period, will allow you special rates. A qualified travel agent will be knowledgeable in these areas.

LOCAL TRAVEL ARRANGEMENTS

When your participants are arriving from a distance within driving range it is helpful to supply them with directions and travel options. Map out various highways and routes and include street directions to the facility. Many people are intimidated by the complexities of one-way streets, no-parking areas, and various signs and laws. This, combined with a time factor, could create unnecessary stress.

Don't take it for granted that people from an area know all their travel options. We are creatures of habit and usually develop patterns and travel habits in which we get stuck. It may never occur to someone who drives to work daily that taking the bus to the seminar could be a relaxing, trouble-free way of traveling. So give them whatever suggestions you have as to options.

In your preseminar communications with the participants, include a facility guide showing such things as restaurants and coffee shops, restrooms, and any other pertinent locations. Include the name of your staff member to whom they can turn for travel assistance. You may also want to include the name of someone at the seminar facility whom they could call for directions or assistance. You may be saying to yourself that this seems to be a lot of work for people who should know their way around their local area. You are right—they should. But do they? Quite often they don't. If only one person is saved from a vexing and unpleasant experience traveling to your seminar, it will be worth the extra effort. The professionalism associated with such attention to detail will be appreciated by those who care. The most important person being you!

NATIONAL
TRAVEL ARRANGEMENTS

When planning national travel arrangements, where can you find help? Here are six ideas:

1. Travel Agents

Listed in Section VI, Where Else Can I Get Help?, are the addresses and telephone numbers of the American Society of Travel Agents (ASTA), and the Association of Retail Travel Agents (ARTA). If you do not have or know a travel agent with whom you can work, these two groups can provide a list from which to choose.

A qualified travel agent can save you untold hours of difficult work. He or she can do all your travel research and suggest alternative plans, and can even help you make a site selection based on either personal experience or transportation information pertinent to the seminar participants.

Whether you are planning to make the travel arrangements for your participants or they will handle their own, consult a travel agent in your advance planning stages for helpful tips.

2. Meeting Planners International

This is a group of highly professional people who make a career of planning and implementing meetings and seminars of every conceivable kind. They have lists and directories of suppliers, including travel consultants. Their address and telephone number is also listed in Where Else Can I Get Help?

3. Airline Sales Offices

Many airlines have people in their local sales office who can give you assistance on such things as group or special rates.

4. Ground Transportation

If your seminar is not in an area serviced by an airline, or if after arriving by airplane the participants must travel by some sort of ground transportation, there are many companies eager for your business. Look them up in the telephone book or call the local chamber of commerce or Visitors' and Convention Bureau.

5. The Seminar Facility

The facility you choose may be a source of assistance. The people there work with a wide range of clients who have similar problems. While you are talking to them, find out what services they provide for transporting your participants to and from the main travel source.

6. Other Seminar Planners

Last but not least are the people you know who have conducted seminars. This is so obvious it is often overlooked.

HOSTS/HOSTESSES

Will you be providing hosts and/or hostesses at the major point of arrival? If so, how many, and how do the participants recognize or contact them? This is important information to include.

POINTS OF INTEREST
AND SPECIAL EVENTS

Include a list of information on points of interest and special events in the area of the seminar facility. If your seminar participants bring spouses or guests, they will appreciate being able to plan some events or entertainment. Many people use a seminar as a vacation and arrive early or stay after for some relaxation and fun.

A checklist or reminder bulletin will be very helpful for your seminar participants. Include a list such as this one in their advance communication package.

PARTICIPANTS' TRAVEL CHECKLIST

Dear Seminar Participant,

Here is a checklist to assist in making your travel arrangements to our seminar. If you have any questions or if we can do anything to make your trip more pleasant, don't hesitate to call.

1. Overnight Accommodations

Hotel/motel, etc.
Type of room
Cost
Reservation number
Arrival—date and time
Departure—date and time

2. Air Travel

Airline
Flight number
Class
Arrival time
Departure time
Cost

3. Automobile

Rental agency
Confirmation number
Cost
Pickup information
Drop-off information

4. Contact People and Telephone Numbers

Facility staff
Seminar staff

5. Travel and Facility Maps and Information

6. Special Clothing

Cold or hot weather
Special events

A final clue for travel arrangements is this: Common sense about travel will always hold you in good stead. If there is a travel problem for or with a participant, just ask yourself, "What would I do in this situation?" Odds are you will have the correct answer.

Ask a Pro

Interview with:
Mr. Larry Wilson
Chairman of the Board, WILSON LEARNING CORPORATION
Eden Prairie, Minnesota

SHEILA: What advice would you give to someone new to the job of staging seminars?

LARRY: This is very general, but I would say to develop their anticipatory skills. I think everything is a matter of anticipation. To me, anticipation means you're ahead of the event or doing what we call potential problem analysis. What might not work? What can we do to get ready for that problem? Combining preventative skills with anticipatory skills is very important in staging seminars.

SHEILA: Is there a single most important item in staging a seminar?

LARRY: No, there are several things that are most important. You need to look for as many ways as possible to present your material. How many ways can you affect the learner or participant? Going for all or as many varied ways of hitting a person's sensory self certainly enhances the opportunity for successful seminars. Look for a seminar facility that can give you as many options as possible.

Another thing is the room setup. When we have a seminar for thirty people or fewer, we always try to set our room in a U-shaped format. The instructor can then move around in the U and be seen by everyone. The participants can also see any flip charts or video we use. This setup gives a more personal atmosphere. People can interact with one another more easily.

SHEILA: In staging seminars, what do you think is the most common mistake?

LARRY: I find that one of the biggest problems is that people just don't plan far enough in advance. They don't have time to do all the creative things that make a seminar really successful. There is very little evaluation or measure done on what took place at the last seminar. So they keep doing the same old things, making the same errors. They don't take time to reassess where they could do better next time.

SHEILA: Do you have a final comment?

LARRY: A final comment would be to use the idea of a mentor. The value of a mentor is that it allows you to go to school on their experience. You don't have to learn it all yourself. It gives you a certain calm and ability to deal with things that may go wrong. You have their experience to back you up. A mentor is a great way to help learn in a shorter time frame.

Ask a Pro

Interview with:

Ms. Fran Lacy

Director of Conference and Institutes, AMERICAN SOCIETY FOR TRAINING AND DEVELOPMENT

Washington, D.C.

SHEILA: What advice would you give to someone new to the job of staging seminars?

FRAN: I would say get to know your suppliers and the people upon whom you will be depending. When you start working with a hotel or conference center, ask them what they need from you. Then keep a constant line of communication open with them. Also, subscribe to as many magazines as you can on the subject. Join groups like the American Society for Training and Development, the American Society of Association Executives, and Meeting Planners International. The key is to work very closely with your own staff and your suppliers, so that everyone can do a better job.

SHEILA: Is there a single most important item in staging a seminar?

FRAN: The key to a successful seminar is communications—finding out your speaker's needs and communicating them to your suppliers. Keep the communications open and flowing between all of your outside suppliers so that there are no surprises at the last minute. Keep the people informed, well in advance, of what you need or expect from them.

SHEILA: In staging seminars, what do you think is the most common mistake?

FRAN: I think many times it's just a lack of innovation, a fear of designing something new, being creative, and using different resources. People seem to be afraid to try new things.

SHEILA: Do you have a final comment?

FRAN: I guess it would be to continue to find the opportunity to work with other people who have been successful at planning seminars. You can learn a lot from them.

chapter thirteen
SEMINAR SITE SELECTION

Selecting a seminar facility location is a costly task, both in terms of time expended and the man-hours and dollars spent in visiting the various locations. But it is necessary and rewarding. Choosing a wrong or inappropriate location can be absolutely disastrous. On the other hand, a facility that fulfills your needs and expectations, has the ambience you require, and gives you good service is not only a joy to work with, but will result in successful staging and logistics of your seminar.

Be sure to review the Train to Success steps. Your choice of location will, of course, be affected by budget, travel arrangements, seminar logistic requirements, seminar style, your personal expectations, and preconceived ideas and concepts.

In this section I will cover the various types of locations available for your seminar. In the following chapter, Facility Requirements, I will cover all the things to look for as you visit the various sites.

Regardless of your needs, don't be afraid to have high expectations in regard to service. As you visit the various locations, be aware of the attitude of the people with whom you will be dealing. If you are ever faced by a choice between a perfect location with a bad or mediocre attitude and a less-than-perfect location with a good attitude, go for the latter. A good service attitude on the part of your seminar facility staff is crucial.

As you shop for a location, don't hesitate to choose a facility that is in an area farther away than you feel is perfect, or that is a little different than what you had in mind. What I'm saying is, go where you are really wanted. In my discussions of suppliers I said that you may decide to use one that you don't particularly like, but who can do the job for you. This is not true in dealing with the facility. Rapport and attitude are very important. In choosing the facility, you should do as I have suggested in choosing your suppliers. Ask other people in your industry what facility they've used. Consult other seminar planners. Hire a consultant, if necessary.

Use all the resources I have suggested, then go shopping. Take your Shopping List Questionnaire, (see Section II, Chapter Four—Suppliers). Be thorough; don't be intimidated by anyone. Your attitude as a professional will be apparent in your thoroughness of questions and your advance preparations. In fact, you may find that you are doing the intimidating with such a thorough list of inquiries and questions.

Realize that very few seminar planners thoroughly research a facility. They think that the facility staff should know what to do. Unfortunately, that is often not the case. You get what you *ask for* and *expect*. That doesn't mean the facilities aren't willing to help you and be cooperative. It means you must be explicit in your questions and descriptions of your needs and expectations.

Before making your on-site inspection, contact the local chamber of commerce and/or Visitors' and Convention Bureau for any information they can provide. Call or write to the various sites you plan to visit and ask for any literature they can provide. Do as much research as possible in advance of your inspection trip.

Here are the general types of sites available to you.

CONVENTION CENTERS

Convention centers usually have large areas available to hold large groups of people, with display and supplier areas. These folks are usually well trained and efficient in staging and logistics. If you are having a large convention or conference where the seminars will be breakout sessions, you may have to use a convention center.

If, however, you are having the seminar as the major or only event, a convention center has some disadvantages. They like to, and are prepared to, sell large blocks of space. They may not want to let you have a small space. It could interfere with an event they may be able to schedule at the same time for a much larger area than yours. They may need your space. Also, you may not want to have a seminar in a location that could have hundreds or thousands of conventioneers in the same location, for obvious reasons.

Another problem might arise from their need to use all their space for the highest dollar return. You may find that you booked the seminar long in advance, agreeing upon a certain room or section to be used. All of a sudden they need the space and ask you to move to a different room or area. You can't be sure the new room will be as good as they say, so you now have a problem. Do you try to find another location? Do you go back and make another inspection? If you don't like the room they have for you, what do you do now?

Always try to be as flexible as possible with any facility you book. They have their side of the story, too. However, your initial choice of a facility should take into account this type of possible problem. Try and have a Plan B just in case, which may mean a secondary choice or space for your seminar at that facility, or it may mean another facility that you could use in an emergency.

So, if you must or want to use a convention center, certainly do so. Just be very clear about what you are getting into, and always have a strong Plan B to fall back on.

CONFERENCE CENTER

There are so many kinds of conference centers that it is difficult to give you a precise description. Each has a variety and range of experience, facility equipment, and capabilities. In researching conference centers, request information and brochures to study before your on-site tour.

Generally, a conference center is one whose primary concern is to conduct conferences, meetings, and seminars for small- to medium-sized groups. Their overnight accommodations usually are not available unless you are also using the conference room facilities. They are well trained in staging and logistics. Your problem arises in researching who has what requirements, experience, length of time in business, etc. How old is their equipment? Can they provide newer, more up-to-date equipment if you need it?

I have been in some conference centers that were built and equipped years ago. They left a lot to be desired. On the other hand, I have been in new facilities that are a speaker/trainer's dream. The range runs to both extremes.

Some conference centers are in quiet areas, away from the metropolitan hustle and bustle. While this may be ideal for your seminar, check the availability of transportation. The center itself is usually well prepared to give you this important information.

Regardless of the age or other factors, I have always had very good experiences with conference centers. They have been eager to please. When presented with a room diagram for setup or other particulars, they were most cooperative. Any facility you choose will have some drawbacks. Conference centers are no different, but they are built and staffed to help you. Don't overlook using a conference center.

HOTELS AND MOTELS

There are more hotels and motels available for seminars than any other type of facility, and they are the most commonly used. There are distinct advantages and disadvantages in using this type of facility. The advantages are:

1. There is a wide choice of facility sizes available in most areas around the country.
2. They are available in a wide price range.
3. They are often close to all sorts of transportation.

The disadvantages are:

1. They are in the business of selling food and beverages and sleeping rooms, not meeting rooms alone.

2. The staff rarely understands how to set up a room (even when presented with a diagram).

3. The service and attitude is so varied (even within a chain of hotels and motels) that you really need to do your homework and have high expectations (and express them).

I have had some perfectly wonderful experiences and some perfectly horrible experiences in hotels and motels. I have come to the conclusion that the facility personnel is more important than the facility itself. You may end up with good examples of both (how lucky!). Let me know and we'll celebrate together.

RESORT AREAS

The very first things to consider if you are thinking of conducting your seminar in a resort area are your seminar objectives and theme.

The advantages and disadvantages of the resort area are quite distinct and may help you decide quickly if you wish to conduct your seminar at such a location.

1. Time of year is important, as you want to be sure that weather and geography do not hinder attendance.

2. Not all resort areas can accommodate the logistics and staging needed for your seminar. This is easy to research. A few questions in an initial phone call or letter will do the job.

3. Resort areas are designed, built, and operated on the "get away, play, and relax" concept. The style and objectives of your seminar will quickly determine how playful and relaxed you want your participants to become.

4. Price. Many resort areas have a package price for meals and sleeping rooms. This may or may not be an advantage. It may be an advantage if the participants are paying for these services themselves and paying you separately for attending the seminar. If your seminar requires overnight accommodations and you are including the costs of room and board in your total seminar fee, then a package price will obviously affect your total budget and the cost to the participants.

5. Resort areas are not generally in locations appropriate for single-day seminars.

Again, contact the local chamber of commerce and/or Visitors' and Convention Bureau in the area you choose to use.

UNIVERSITIES, COLLEGES, AND SCHOOLS

Educational facilities may also make your decisions easy. They elicit a programmed response from people, whether your seminar participants were excellent students or poor students, whether they liked going to school or not. The response is the same to a structured environment.

The flexibility for room setup is usually narrow. The range of equipment is as wide as conference center equipment.

Universities, colleges, and schools almost never have facilities for refreshments or coffee breaks. If your seminar requires overnight accommodations, you must check carefully. They may have dormitories or similar arrangements. The way our youngsters live in dorms between the ages of eighteen and twenty is a lot different than most of us will be comfortable with even for one or two nights. Educational facilities are best suited for a single-day seminar or a drive in for more than a one-day type of seminar.

CRUISE SHIPS

Cruise ships are a light, relaxing change of pace. Everything is supplied for you: food, entertainment, accommodations, and tons of attention. Most cruise lines welcome your business and are very cooperative and anxious to please. There are those that offer you a free trip when a certain number of people are booked, so you may have a paid vacation while working. Cruise ships are fun, but the biggest problem is that they require large cash deposits to hold space for your participants. Your budget is a large consideration here.

The atmosphere is not highly conducive to a serious subject. But depending upon who is attending and your objectives, this may be a fun alternative. Check carefully the rulings for tax deductions before taking someone's word for the fact that the seminar costs may be deductible aboard a cruise ship. There are some new laws that have been passed and you need to be aware of them.

COUNTRY CLUBS, TOWN HALLS, CHURCHES, AND CONFERENCE ROOMS

This is the do-it-yourself setting. The local chamber of commerce is a great resource for small seminars calling for these types of rooms. You will probably need to bring in most of your own equipment and services. They may have a kitchen area and a few supplies, like coffeepots, but basically you are on your own. They are often in quiet, pleasant locations and can be a very welcome change of pace.

These are excellent for seminars with small budgets and people who are just beginning to market public seminars. As long as you use a detailed flow chart and checklist and are willing to do it yourself, these facilities can be very nice.

IN-HOUSE FACILITIES

Whether you are a seminar speaker/trainer and have been hired to conduct a seminar for a company, or you work within a company, corporation, or group, there are several things to keep in mind. When conducting seminars in-house:

1. Be very clear about what equipment and materials you require. It can cause a great deal of confusion in the building if last-minute problems arise. This confusion is never appreciated by those *not* attending the seminar.

2. Try and use a room or rooms as far away from the participants' work area as possible. It is a never-ending problem for participants to be tempted to make "just one phone call."

3. Supervisors and executives often drop in and kibitz, which intimidates and interrupts the participants. They also know where their subordinates are, and may feel tempted to call them out of the seminar to handle a problem.

I would always suggest taking the participants out of their everyday working location. They are free of distractions and disturbances; their attention span is longer; and most of all, they feel special when they get to "go" to a seminar. Attitude is always important. The extra cost of renting outside facilities seems to pay off in acceptance and retention of seminar materials and ideas.

The eight types of facilities listed cover a vast majority of seminar locations. You can be assured that if you do your homework in advance, make on-site inspections, use your Shopping List Questionnaire, and observe carefully the attitude of those people you will be working with at the facility, you will probably make a wise choice. If, however, at the conclusion of the seminar you find that you made a mistake in choosing that particular facility, take your lumps. Learn as much as possible from your mistake and research another facility for the next time.

Ask a Pro

Interview with.
Mr. D. John Hammond
President, AMERICAN MOTIVATIONAL ASSOCIATION
Scottsdale, Arizona

SHEILA: What advice would you give to someone new to the job of staging seminars?

JOHN: The best advice I can give to anyone new to the job of staging seminars is never to assume anyone will perform as they have promised. Always check everything for yourself.

SHEILA: Is there a single most important item in staging a seminar?

JOHN: I think there is not just one most important item, but four. They are:

1. Send a detailed chart or drawing of the room setup well in advance of your arrival at the facility. Then go to the workers who will actually be doing the setup the night before and go over the diagram.

2. Lighting in a theatrical setting, such as an auditorium with fixed seating and a built-in stage, will probably be quite sufficient, and available. However, if you are in a facility that only has regular room lighting, you may want to have them rent or bring in extra lighting so that you can have the front of the room well lit.

3. Controlling participants' seating can often be a problem. If you are using a hotel facility you can set the room for less than you expect. Therefore,

all the seats will be filled. You can then add seats in the back of the room as people arrive. That way you don't have empty seats and people spread out all over the room.

4. If you are using a facility such as an auditorium or a room with fixed seating and you don't want to have the people spread out, there's an easy, inexpensive trick to try. Go to an office-supply firm and purchase rolls of adding machine tape, then take this tape and "rope off" the areas you don't want used.

SHEILA: In staging seminars, what do you think is the most common mistake?
JOHN: There are several I've noted:

1. Typically, when using slides, people have someone in the room operating the slide equipment. So there is always a lag with "Next slide," or "You can go on to the next one." This conversation between the speaker/trainer and assistant is distracting, slows down the presentation, and looks and sounds unprofessional.

    Here is a tip that works nicely. The speaker should develop a body language cue that sends the signal that means "Next slide, please." A simple gesture will do, such as raising the right hand slightly, or anything that will be a key signal that the assistant recognizes.

2. One of the worst mistakes is not making friends with the facility manager. Get him or her on your side. Make this person feel important (because they are). He or she will go to bat for you on such things as room setup, lighting, etcetera.

3. When shipping materials to a facility, mark the boxes carefully with the names of the people to receive them, not just the facility name. Then take some tape, labels, and kindergarten-type scissors along with you so that you will be able to ship the materials back to your home base. People quite often forget to bring these little tools with them.

4. Note to speakers/trainers:
    To sell or not to sell product—don't surprise the group hiring you. Make any and all arrangements for product sales in advance. Don't ever surprise them. That is a good way to ruin your reputation and to cause disharmony.

SHEILA: Do you have a final comment?
JOHN: I would suggest that if you put on seminars for the general public in the evening, make arrangements to hire a security guard to be in attendance. You will be surprised how many problems might be avoided by simply having that person obviously visible.

    My final comment would be, go back to square one! Don't assume anyone will do what they promise. Life is a do-it-yourself project, and so is conducting seminars.

chapter fourteen
FACILITY REQUIREMENTS

You are at a major decision point in the planning and implementation of your seminar.

You have established your theme, set certain policies, designated tasks, started flow charts and checklists. You've begun budget planning, and selected a time frame in which to hold your seminar. You've begun the travel research process and have selected or begun the selection process of the speaker/trainer. You have decided upon the style and room setup theme that you would like to use. You have researched the various types of facilities in which to conduct the seminar.

These preparations, however, cannot be completed until you finalize the selection of a seminar facility.

In the previous section we have covered the types of facilities most often used for seminars. The pros and cons have been touched upon. You have generally decided upon two or three—or perhaps as many as a dozen—sites to visit and inspect. But don't leave yet!

The time and money you spend on your inspection tour will be wisely spent or poorly spent, depending upon the amount of homework you have done before you leave.

1. Consult, review, and work with any of your staff members who will be directly affected by your selection of the facility. Do they have questions

or requirements you will need to clarify and confirm during your on-site inspection?

2. Summarize your notes and any information you have received from each of the facilities.

I assume that by now you have researched the prospective sites and come up with facts such as this: Your seminar will have approximately five hundred people and the facility's largest room holds three hundred, or your seminar will have twenty people and the smallest room they have available holds five hundred.

Red lights should go off in your head. Careful! Don't waste time and money visiting inappropriate locations.

3. Review this entire section. Develop questions that will apply to your seminar's specifics. Then turn to Section IV, The Seminar. In that section I cover in detail such things as registration. You will need to be aware of the entire process of registration before you visit the site. There are questions that will occur to you for your on-site inspections, such as whether there is an area outside the seminar room large enough to accommodate your registration needs. I will cover these types of items in a general fashion in this section. You need to look for specifics that apply to your seminar so that you will have a full and complete list of questions.

AN OVERVIEW

Questions to ask yourself—points to ponder:

- Does this facility lend itself, in an overall fashion, to the theme, objectives, subject matter, and presentation of your seminar?
- Do you wish to follow a standard format for your seminar? Or would you like to try something more innovative? Does this location provide that difference or flexibility? Does this facility lend itself to your innovative ideas?
- Do you wish to retain a standard seminar presentation, but provide an innovative or unique facility/setting? Does this facility fill the bill?
- Is the general decor and atmosphere complementary to your seminar purpose? Consider such things as disquieting colors; too many mirrors, which distract attention; ill-placed pillars in the seminar room, which break visual contact with participants; dark or windowless rooms that give a tomblike effect.

These are several factors that can play a very important subconscious role in the overall success of the seminar:

- Have you considered the economic, educational, ethnic, and religious backgrounds of your participants? Does this facility lend itself to their special needs (e.g., dietary)? Do you see any clue of discriminatory practices?

As you consider the overall features, benefits, and liabilities, there are two times to take a wide general view of each facility. The first is when you arrive and take a cursory look around. Remember, your first impression will be the same as that of your participants. Does the facility project an image you can be proud of?

Arrive early enough to take a walk around the facility before your meetings with the staff. Ask questions of people conducting meetings or seminars, such as: How was the housekeeping crew? Did they do a good job? Was the front desk helpful and pleasant? Did the setup crew work with you?

The second overview should come at the end of your tour. After the question-and-answer session with the facility staff, and after going into details about your seminar requirements, is this facility more or less attractive? How do you feel now that you have met the staff and discussed your special needs?

At these two times you might get a gut reaction. Listen carefully to your instincts. As you become more experienced in seminaring, these instincts play an important role.

Now that you have an overview, let's go on to more specific items.

ENTRANCES, EXITS, ELEVATORS, STAIRS, AND RAMPS

Are the entrances, exits, elevators, stairs, and ramps well lit and designated? Will these easily accommodate the size of your group? Are there accommodations for the handicapped?

OVERNIGHT ACCOMMODATIONS

If your seminar requires you, your staff, and/or participants to stay overnight, there are several questions to ask.

1. Do you need to guarantee a certain number of sleeping rooms to get a reduced rate or no-charge rate for the seminar rooms? If so, how many sleeping rooms are required? How much reduction in the seminar room costs will be given, if any?

2. What is the cancellation policy if you don't use all of the sleeping rooms you're committed to? What are the cancellation deadlines on sleeping rooms? How will this affect seminar room costs, if at all?

3. Is an advance deposit required on sleeping rooms? If so, how much and when is it due?

4. Are there on-season or off-season rates? What are they? When do the seasons begin and end?

5. Do they give a corporate discount? Are you eligible for this?

6. Will they give a discount on the sleeping rooms if you use a certain number? If so, how many are required to qualify and how much discount do they give? This is different from question 1. In question 1 I was referring to the number of sleeping rooms required to get a reduction in the charges for the seminar room. Here you are asking if they will give you a discount in sleeping rooms if you use a certain number.

7. Will your seminar participants get a special rate if they share a room? This may make the difference as to whether someone can afford to attend.

8. If you have a large enough group to fill the entire facility and you need an overflow accommodation, do they have a cooperative agreement with other facilities nearby? If so, what is the agreement? How do you control—or work with them in controlling—the overflow?

9. Do the sleeping rooms have the flexibility to be used as small meeting rooms or breakout rooms or reception rooms, if necessary?

10. What is the range of accommodations? What is the price range?

    Single rooms—twin, three-quarter, or double beds
    Double rooms—double, queen- or king-size beds (three or more people might share this room).
    Accommodations for children—cots, cribs, playpens, etc.
    Deluxe rooms
    Junior suites
    Suites

    If you are bringing in a large group for the seminar and will be using a large number of their sleeping rooms, do they give "comp" (complimentary) low-fee or no-fee deluxe rooms or suites to the seminar executives, directors, or planners?

11. Have you actually seen the variety of rooms? Do you like them? Would *you* like to stay in them?

12. Are the sleeping rooms located in an easy traffic pattern to the seminar room or rooms? Will it be a problem for participants to go back and forth to their rooms when necessary?

13. Are the sleeping rooms near noisy public areas such as swimming pools, bars, lounges, dining rooms, elevators, outside noises, or the street? If so, how many rooms are located near these noises? Will the noises affect a good night's rest for your participants?

14. It also makes a difference whether you are including the accommodations in the price of the seminar. If so, you will make the decision yourself as to whether you like the rooms. If the participants are paying separately for their sleeping rooms, they will want as wide a choice as you can provide.

15. Alternative accommodations are another question to ask about. Regarding overnight accommodations you will want to know whether, if your participants use all the sleeping rooms available in the facility and some must be located in other facilities nearby, does the seminar facility provide a shuttle service to transport the participants back and forth? If not, how will you accomplish this task? Cabs, car rentals, buses, vans? Who will organize and coordinate the service? Be sure to check parking facilities. Are they nearby and adequate?

FOOD AND REFRESHMENTS

When you call to make the appointment for an on-site inspection you will need to set time aside for the catering manager or food and beverage manager. Set an exact time so there is no chance that he or she will be out or not available for your meeting. Some sales departments also do the food and beverage arrangements. Even then I would ask to discuss your needs with someone involved with, if not the head of, the food and beverage or catering department. This subject is covered in detail in Section IV, The Seminar. Review it carefully for the questions you should ask. This is one of the most crucial subjects in this book. The mistakes made are always costly not only in money, but in time and the comfort and convenience of your seminar participants. This section on food and beverages can make or break a profit margin.

Do your homework. Take nothing for granted. Question everything. Put *every* detail in writing and check, recheck and double-check all of the food and beverage requirements.

CONTACT PEOPLE
AND FACILITY STAFF

As you progress through your on-site inspection, make a detailed list of the facility's staff and department heads whom you will be working with. When you have made your decision of which facility to use, keep the information on the other sites you inspected. You never know when you may have occasion to use one of the other facilities. You may have to use Plan B if something goes wrong with your first choice of facility sites. It will save you a lot of time if you already have the names, addresses, and telephone numbers of other facilities and staff.

List their names, titles, telephone numbers, and their departments. If they are located outside of the main facility, find out if you need a secondary address for written communications. List the hours they work—i.e., morning shift, weekend shift, etc.

In the case of a department head, find out who is the second in command. Share with both of these people your seminar flow chart and checklist that is appropriate for their department. The more information you share with them on key points, time frames, and personal expectations, the better equipped they will be to help you.

Communicate everything in writing to all department heads and stay in very close touch with them as you progress through your planning stages and into the actual presentation of the seminar. Let them know that you are aware of their responsibilities and accountability; express your willingness to work with them. This will help eliminate a great deal of stress associated with seminar preparation and implementation.

NOISES AND SOUNDS

As you conduct your on-site inspection, take time to tour the entire facility by yourself. Listen to noises and sounds that may be distracting during the actual presentation of the seminar. There are many noises and sounds to be aware of:

1. Where is the kitchen or catering area in relation to your seminar room or rooms? Kitchen and catering staff are not very sympathetic to your

needs if they are serving in other rooms and your seminar is located near their work area.

2. Where are the access halls to the kitchen or catering areas, storage areas, nonpublic areas? These areas can be very noisy and terribly distracting to seminar participants. You just don't need to compete with these kinds of noisy areas.

3. What functions are planned in an adjacent area or nearby rooms? In many facilities a large ballroom or open area intended to handle large functions can be divided into smaller areas. These areas are used as separate rooms, and several functions can be accommodated at once. The dividing walls (some attached separately, some permanently attached) expand across the width of the large area. They look nice and often appear permanent. The problem is, they are rarely as soundproof as the facility would have you believe. Be sure to find out the who, what, where, when, why, and how of functions in rooms or areas adjoining your seminar.

4. Where are the public ingress and egress areas? Will the doors to your seminar room be in the path of public traffic? People unthinkingly, or unknowingly, open doors and pop their heads in looking for someone or something. This can be very disturbing to your seminar. There is absolutely no way to control the noise in public ingress or egress areas. Try to avoid rooms located near these areas.

5. Are there coffee shops, snack bars, restaurants, cocktail lounges nearby? If there are, what are their serving hours? Are they close enough to your seminar room to create noise problems? If your seminar extends into the evening, be particularly careful. You don't need to have a jukebox, rock band, or other entertainment source near your seminar room.

6. Does the facility have a swimming pool, sauna, Jacuzzi, exercise area, or tennis courts? If so, where are they located? What time do they open and close? Will there be noise from them that could affect the seminar?

SMELLS, AROMAS, AND ODORS

Take a walk around and through the facility and see what you can smell.

1. Are the rest rooms clean and free of odor? Where are they located in relation to your seminar room?

2. Where are the facility garbage cans or dumpsters? Will their odors be a problem?

3. Kitchen smells, both good and bad, can be distracting. If the aromas from

the kitchen are delicious and your participants are hungry, it can be very distracting; obviously, the opposite also applies.

This section on smells, aromas, and odors is a small item, but well worth a few minutes of your time.

KITCHENS AND CATERING AREAS

We have discussed these areas in terms of noise and smells. There are other points to look for and inquire about.

If you are serving refreshments or meals, the ideal situation is to have the catering or kitchen area close enough to serve and clear quickly and to let you begin or finish quickly. But if the kitchen is too close, it can be a problem in the noise and smell area.

If you need extra refreshments at a break, it is not always easy to find a facility staff member to assist you. It's handy to be able to walk back to the food-preparation area and ask for someone there to help. Or in a do-it-yourself location, it is nice to be close enough to take care of the problem yourself quickly. Many facilities have the kitchens or catering areas in a main location. They then use smaller serving areas from which to hold and serve the food. There are some pluses and minuses to this arrangement. The plus is that there is usually less noise and distraction; the minus is that if you need extra anything, it is not always quickly available (if at all)! Also, food can get cold, or hot, depending on the weather, while being transported from the main preparation area.

Your specific needs will dictate the extent and use of catering and kitchen areas.

COFFEE SHOPS,
RESTAURANTS, AND SNACK BARS

If your seminar does not call for refreshments or food service, or if you do not plan to include these, you need to research some information for the convenience of your participants.

1. Does this facility have food service accommodations, such as coffee shops, restaurants, or snack bars?
2. What hours do they serve?
3. Can they accommodate special dietary needs?
4. What is their price range?
5. What are the accepted methods of payment? Cash, check, credit card (if credit cards are accepted, which ones)?
6. Does the facility have a locator map that you can include in the information packet for participants in regard to these eating facilities?

If you wish to provide an open-bar arrangement for the participants, this means that the facility will provide refreshments just for your group in an area close to the seminar. The participants pay for their purchases themselves and don't have to leave the seminar area. Not all facilities can provide this service, but be sure and check. It is a good middle-ground arrangement for the participants' comfort and convenience if you are not providing the refreshments or food service.

If the facility does not have public food service available, research the who, what, where, when, and how of local eating establishments. Research all the same questions listed above for the facility eating places. Then find out about transportation information, such as, how do participants get back and forth from these public eating establishments, the costs involved, the length of time involved, etc. You may want to go so far as to provide a description of the type of food served or a menu for each of the various establishments. In any event, research how your participants can best fill their needs for food and refreshments.

A last resort, but also acceptable, is the possibility that the facility may have vending machines near the seminar room or ones that can be brought in for some quick refreshments.

Ask a Pro

Interview with:
Ms. Dottie Walters
President, ROYAL CBS PUBLISHING
Glendora, California

SHEILA: What advice would you give to someone new to the job of staging seminars?

DOTTIE: I would tell them, "Don't assume anything, don't take anything for granted, triple-check everything—you can't be too careful!" You must be very, very thorough. The successful seminars always have people managing them who are meticulous. Another suggestion for those who have any product sales at the seminar is to be sure and have a helper. If you are the seminar leader, you can't answer questions, sign autographs, sell the product all at one time! You definitely need a helper.

SHEILA: Is there a single most important item in staging a seminar?

DOTTIE: I think the most important things are the noise, lighting, and air-conditioning factors. These must be checked out far in advance to make sure there aren't such things as music coming through the facility music/announcing system. You need to question such things as lawn-mowing day, or what the local road department has planned in that area. You need to be sure your seminar room is not in competition with another seminar or event. Are you next to a room that will be noisy? You need to check to be sure your room is not adjacent to the bar or a social eating and drinking area. I think being aware of these factors is the most important success component in conducting a seminar. If it is too dark to see, too noisy to hear, and too hot to think, it is hard to be successful.

SHEILA: In staging seminars, what do you think is the most common mistake?

DOTTIE: One of the things that people forget about or perhaps think is not a major item is a very important problem. Make sure the seminar is not scheduled on a national or local holiday or during a special event in the particular area where the seminar is being held. It can make a major impact on the attendance at your seminar. This is essential. Seminars being conducted in competition with this type of event have disastrous results! No one shows up.

SHEILA: Do you have a final comment?

DOTTIE: Yes. I have had many wonderful people who have acted as mentors to me. Find a mentor who is experienced and will advise you in putting on successful seminars. Don't be shy about asking questions. As Plato said, "People are like iron rings. When one is magnetized it has the power to touch another and magnetize it, too." People who are successful are glad to help others. The bigger the name, the more generous they become. So do yourself a favor and find a mentor. My own mentor, Ben Franklin, said, "Experience keeps an expensive school, a fool will learn in no other." And remember, when you have been a protégé, it is then your obligation to "pass it on" and be a mentor to others who need help.

TELEPHONES

Public Telephones

The best arrangement for public telephones is to have them located far enough from the seminar room so as not to cause noise from people traffic, but close enough for participants to use conveniently.

I try to locate a seminar room just far enough away from the phones so that it is slightly inconvenient to use them, thus helping the participants resist the temptation to run in and out making "just one more call."

If your facility does not have a public telephone available, research the nearest location of one (without walking a great distance, if possible). Make a note of which telephones accept coins only or credit cards only, and which will accept both.

In-house Telephones

If you are using a facility that will provide various services, it is crucial to have an in-house telephone in or very near the facility location or room. If the in-house phone is in the seminar room, check the loudness of the ring so you can plan to have someone nearby during the seminar. If messages need to be sent to the seminar room, you don't want the phone ringing off and on and causing a disturbance.

REST ROOMS

As you tour the facility, check the rest rooms to be sure that they are clean, well-stocked, well-lit, and that they will be unlocked during the seminar hours.

If you are using a very large facility, inquire as to locator signs that may be placed for speedy use of the rest rooms during the seminar.

If the facility you are using is a college campus and your seminar will be on a weekend, find out who is responsible for the locking, unlocking, and care of the rest rooms. You don't want to arrive in the morning of your seminar and have no rest rooms open. This once happened to me in a junior college; it took all morning to get someone there to finally unlock the rest rooms. Campus security and maintenance are rarely available at times other than regular weekday hours to lend this kind of assistance. Churches and all other types of nonprofessional facilities should be checked out very carefully regarding these arrangements and use of rest room facilities.

STENOGRAPHIC SERVICES AND COPYING FACILITIES

At the time of your seminar you may need to make copies of items or materials or make use of a stenographic service. Check with the facility to see if they have a copy machine on the premises and also if they have stenographic services available. If so, what hours are they available? If these services are not available, inquire as to where is the nearest location for these services that can be conveniently used by you and your staff.

Compare prices at the seminar facility, if the services are available there, and at the nearby location. Keep the information on hand in your planner's manual.

DISABLED PARTICIPANTS' NEEDS

If there will be disabled persons attending your seminar (or if you don't know), check the facility's capabilities to make these people comfortable. Ask yourself these questions:

- Does this facility have ramps?
- Are the rest rooms equipped properly?
- Are doors wide enough to accommodate a wheelchair?
- Do the buildings have elevators?
- Are there automobile parking spaces for the disabled?
- Are the drinking fountains low enough for a person in a wheelchair to use?
- Are the telephones low enough for a person in a wheelchair to use?

Some new facilities even have the elevator floor-selection numbers printed in Braille for blind persons. While you certainly wouldn't eliminate a facility because it didn't have Braille elevator buttons, you do need to be aware of the comfort of your disabled participants.

It is a terribly frustrating experience for disabled persons to try to function in a facility that is careless or thoughtless of their needs.

SEMINAR ROOM SELECTION

Before you arrive for your on-site inspection, you have decided:

1. What style of room setup you wish to use for the seminar.
2. If you will need breakout rooms (rooms adjacent to the main seminar room) for before, during, or after the seminar:
   A. *Before*—could be a registration area; a reception, welcoming, or social area.
   B. *During*—could be for subgroup work related to the main seminar.
   C. *After*—could be for postreception, evaluation session, or departure waiting area.
3. How many people do you plan to have in attendance?
4. If you plan refreshment breaks or food service.
5. What the speaker/trainer needs are in relation to the actual seminar presentation and room.

You should by now have a list of questions to ask and requirements that need to be fulfilled for seminar room selection.

Here are a few additional points regarding choice of a seminar room. These have not been covered in the previous sections.

Room Location

Check this in reference to the entrances and exits. Is the room you choose conveniently located to the entrances, exits, elevators, and stairs? Does it make a big difference to you? If your group is small (forty people or under), it may not matter if there is only one elevator available, or that the entrance and exit is not very close. However, if your group is large—several hundred people, for instance—it will make a big difference if you have only one elevator available to your seminar room. The time delays in bringing people up and down can have a massive effect on the smooth flow of your seminar.

I once ran into this exact problem. I had five hundred people attending a seminar. The only way to the second floor and the seminar room was by using the stairs or using the only elevator in the building. It caused many delays. We started late, refreshment breaks were late, the lunch was delayed, and people were irritated at having to wait for the elevator or being forced to use the stairs. As I look back, it also occurs to me that it was probably a fire code infraction to have so few exits for so many people.

If you will be having a large group it may also cause delays if the entrances and exits are a long distance from the seminar location. If this is the case, allow extra time for registration. Build in a time safety factor.

Registration Area

Does the room you choose for the seminar have a comfortable, convenient registration area? Or will you need to use a breakout room for the registration area? Will you need to use the seminar room itself for registration, and if so, is it large enough to serve both functions comfortably? (See Section IV, Chapter 2—Registration—for details.)

Refreshment Breaks and Food Service

Are you planning on serving refreshments before or during the seminar? If so, can you use the seminar room? Do you need a hallway or breakout room? Are they large enough and available?

If you will be serving a meal or meals, will you be using the seminar room for these food functions? Buffet luncheons can be served and participants can dine at the same tables they use during the seminar. Or, if the room is large enough, dividers can be placed so that half of the room is used for the seminar and the other half is used for the food service. This often works out quite nicely, it gives a feeling of self-containment and continuity.

If you will be using another room for food service, where will it be located? A room adjacent to the seminar room also gives you a feeling of continuity. If you use a room removed from the seminar area, it gives continuity but with a little more break in intensity.

I have used both types of food-service rooms. The seriousness and depth of the seminar material will help you decide whether you wish to give the participants a small or large mental and emotional break.

Of course, if you do not provide food or refreshments, the participants are on their own. Suggestions on this possibility are discussed in the preceding section entitled Coffee Shops, Restaurants, and Snack Bars.

Room Size

The number of participants and setup style will determine the size of room required for your seminar.

As you begin discussing the size of the room you will need, find out how the facility measures room capacity. Do they measure their seating capacity by theater style (chairs only), classroom style (tables and chairs), or banquet style (tables set for waiters and waitresses to move between, either round tables or long tables)?

You can waste a lot of time discussing which rooms to use if the facility person is thinking in terms of classroom style and you are thinking in terms of round tables. Whether to use a large room or small room can be a perplexing question.

A large room used for a small group can provide an open, spread-out feeling. Again, your seminar style will determine how tight (closely set) you want the room. If you are forced to use a room larger than you want, room dividers can give it more intimacy and closeness by sectioning off the room for the size you desire. The unused portion of the room, as stated before, might be used for registration or refreshment breaks.

Smaller rooms, or one that is filled to capacity, will give a more intimate, dynamic feeling. A room set tight (but not crowded) is preferable to one that is spread out. The participants' attention may wander if the room is set too loosely, with too much open space. If you will remember that a 10 percent no-show rate is average, you can judge your room capacity more effectively. If your seminar will have twenty people, that 10 percent (two people) no-show rate probably doesn't mean too much. However, if you are planning to have two hundred people in attendance, the 10 percent (twenty people) can make a much bigger difference. So keep the 10 percent in mind when you decide on the size of your seminar room.

Color Scheme and General Room Ambience

Consider the color of the room and the general decor. A bright red velvet wall covering may be delightful for a dinner or a banquet, but it will have a negative effect on participants if they must sit in the room all day. The color red has proven to be stressful and less than conducive to concentration and learning. Neutral and earth-tone colors are best for seminar rooms. Also observe the ceiling height of the room—it can make a big difference. If the room has a low ceiling and a very busy wallpaper pattern, the room will feel crowded very quickly. On the other hand, a high-ceilinged room with neutral walls would give a more open feeling.

If you have any choice, select a room that is carpeted. This will help with noise and general comfort. Decoration should be free of distraction, such as mirrors, pillars, paintings, busy wallpaper, and chandeliers.

Lighting

The type and style of your seminar will determine the kind of lighting you do or do not wish to use. Three factors to consider are:

> You do not want the content of the seminar to compete with the present lighting in the seminar room. Lighting that is either too dim or too bright is unsatisfactory. Too bright a room gives the feeling of an assembly plant. Too dim a room feels like a cocktail lounge. Ask the facility to change the wattage if the lights are too dim. Hopefully, they can accommodate a higher wattage.

> As you walk around in the proposed seminar room, try to picture the seminar leader in action. There should be some extra lighting on the leader other than just normal room lights. Facial expression, body language, flip charts, blackboards, and any sort of communication tools need to be seen clearly by all of the participants. The

use of floodlights on the S/T is far more desirable than spotlights, because spotlights are very hot and difficult to work under for any length of time.

Does your seminar require black lights or special lighting for multimedia presentations or any special effects? Be sure to discuss all your special lighting needs during the on-site inspection tour. If new or additional lighting becomes an apparent need in your planning process, contact the facility immediately. Don't walk in the day before or the day of the seminar and ask for special equipment. Give the facility time to prepare and assist you with the proper lighting.

There are several general areas regarding lighting that you need to be aware of during your site selection process. Is there proper lighting in the parking facilities and along outside walkways? Is there proper lighting in the lobby, hallways, and rest rooms?

Any area that your participants will be using should be well lit, not only for safety, but for cheerfulness and general appearance.

Audiovisual Needs

The chapter on audiovisual equipment in Section II, Advance Work, goes into much more detail as to what kind of specific audiovisual equipment you may need. For the purpose of room selection, be sure that:

1. There are adequate electrical outlets and that they are located where you need them.
2. That the amplification system can handle your needs. Ask to have a microphone brought into the room and then try it out to be sure that you like the sound system.
3. If they don't have the type of microphone or any other audiovisual equipment you need, find out:
   A. Will they rent it for you?
   B. Do they have someone available to assist you should you need help with the audiovisual equipment?
   C. Are there charges for audiovisual staff or equipment (rented or owned by them)?

There are no standard answers for these questions. Some facilities will provide general audiovisual equipment such as microphones, lecterns, or freestanding speakers at no cost to you. Others will charge you for everything, including such items as extension cords, so be sure you understand their policy on audiovisual equipment. Remember, everything is negotiable.

Some facilities will allow you to bring in your own equipment and use it. Others will allow you to bring it in, but once it is on the premises they require a staff member to work, set up, and operate the equipment. Yet others will not allow you to bring anything in or even operate the equipment yourself. It is reasonable to have a facility require a staff person to operate the microphone system, large viewing screens, etc., so don't try to save money by doing these larger jobs yourself (supervise them if you wish to and are familiar enough to do so). However, it is unreasonable to require you to pay facility staff personnel to plug in an extension cord or operate a projector for you. Be sure that you negotiate these types of requirements.

You will not believe how many different sets of rules there are in the various parts of the country regarding audiovisual equipment and operation. So be sure to ask all these types of questions.

Risers and Stages

By definition, risers and stages are quite different. A stage is for entertainment; it has a theatrical effect on the seminar participants. Stages are usually high enough off the ground so the front row of people must be set back several feet. This leaves a vacant area between the person on the stage and the people in the audience and gives a set-apart feeling.

Risers, on the other hand, do just that—they raise someone or something off the ground just enough for clear viewing, but not so high as to cause cramped necks and that set-apart feeling. Before deciding to use risers or stages, consider the presentation style of the seminar leader. Is it one of teacher, entertainer, expert, sharer of ideas? Is it casual and relaxed: Is it that of a facilitator rather than lecturer?

When using stages and risers in a seminar, do so carefully. The size of your seminar may require a riser so that everyone can see the speaker as well as any audiovisual equipment used. However, risers and stages can create physical barriers where you may not want them. Again, the style of your seminar presentation will determine the use of risers and stages. Just make sure that all participants have a clear view of what you want them to see.

If the speaker is to be an expert or celebrity, a stage or riser will enhance this effect. You can use it to great advantage. A little showmanship is often called for.

If the proposed room has a permanently fixed stage and you want to use it, check these things in advance:

1. Do the curtains open and close easily?
2. Are they manually or electronically operated?
3. Is the stage surface clean, squeaky, safe to use?
4. Where are the steps or ramps located and are they readily accessible and clean?
5. If you are using dressing rooms, where are they located and are they readily accessible and clean?
6. Are the outlets on the stage easily available for your audiovisual equipment?
7. Are you required to use stagehands or can you use the part of the stage that is directly in front of the curtain only (therefore avoiding fees for stagehands, etc.)?
8. What are the lighting arrangements? Can you handle them yourself or do you need special lighting people on hand?
9. Last, but not least, is the stage really large enough for your purpose? Or is it too large? You don't want your speaker or trainer looking like he or she fell in a hole somewhere on an enormous stage.

In considering whether to use risers or stages and/or what size or style to use, take an overall view from the participants' place in the audience. Consider their comfort and ability to see. Also consider the speaker/trainer's ability to communicate with them through the proper room setting, using risers and/or stages.

NEGOTIATING WITH THE FACILITY

You have made your on-site tour and are ready to sit down and discuss your needs.

You will receive better service and treatment and can negotiate better prices if you can book the seminar at a time during which the facility needs to fill space and therefore create income. Sit down with a general idea in mind of when you'd like to have the seminar. Then let them know that you understand from where their income is derived (sleeping rooms and food and beverage), and that you'd be happy to work with them on a time that is not being held for a larger or more profitable group. Let them know that you also expect some deductions in costs for your flexibility. They will know you understand how the game is played. If you are in a facility that is always busy, be as flexible as possible. It will be appreciated.

If *you* are the big group they are looking for, then you have a whole different kind of clout. For example, seminar rooms are seldom charged for when you provide the facility with a generous income from sleeping rooms and/or food and beverage service along with the use of the seminar room or rooms. When negotiating, try to deal with the highest authority possible. What person at the facility makes the final decision on financial quotes, time and space available, etc.? That's the person you want to deal with.

If this is your first experience at planning a seminar, be honest; tell them that. Ask for their help and assistance. Don't bluff. Facility salespeople deal with potential clients every single day, and they recognize a novice from a pro. You'll have a much happier experience if it is begun with candor.

If this is not your first seminar, be prepared to have information about your previous seminars available for the prospective facility. For example:

1. How many seminar rooms did you use for your last seminar?
2. How many people did you plan to have in attendance? How many actually attended?
3. How many sleeping rooms did you set aside? How many were actually used?
4. How many meals or refreshments were ordered? How many did you actually use?
5. What facility was your last seminar held at and how do you feel about their services, etc.?

It has become common practice for one facility to call another and ask about your previous events, payments or charges, and so forth. They take this information into account when making financial arrangements with you (of course, don't forget you let them know by your flow charts and checklists that you are a pro and know what you are doing). Let them know that you will also check *them* out. (Remember your Shopping List Questionnaire; ask questions like, Who has used your services before? and so on.)

FINANCIAL ARRANGEMENTS

When you've negotiated the best price for the best services and have decided upon your seminar facility, it is time to make your financial arrangements.

You should by now have an idea of the going rates for what you will need from the facility. Depending upon your background and the background of your group, you will have certain choices for the financial arrangements.

If you are an entrepreneur and this is your first public seminar, you may have to make a deposit on some of the services. At the very least you will have to sign an agreement guaranteeing the number of attendees for such things as meal service, and perhaps other services.

You will probably need to pay the final bill at the conclusion of the event. (After you establish a financial track record with the facility you can usually set up a line of credit. Then the payments can be made by a prescribed date following the seminar.) You may also be required to fill out a financial statement to assure them that you will be able to pay the bill.

If, however, you are planning a group of seminars and your company is a multimillion-dollar concern, it will be easier to establish credit and negotiate prices.

In any case, be very careful that your financial arrangements coincide with your budget expenditures and time frames (e.g., your budget shows that X amount of people need to prepay their registration by a certain date to coincide with the deposit to the facility, but you inadvertently set the deposit date a month before your preregistration date).

A financial arrangement to be aware of if you plan to sell product at your seminar is this: Many facilities will require a certain percentage of the gross sales for allowing you to sell product on the premises.

Ask—if this is the case, be sure you have a very clear, precise amount established. You should always try and negotiate this downward, or perhaps use another facility.

EXCHANGING CONTRACTS

There is such a variety of opinions on the best method of using contracts that it is mind boggling. There is no perfect way.

If your seminar is complicated and very expensive, it is a good idea to seek legal advice on any contract used with suppliers and facilities.

However, if your seminar is straightforward and of a general nature, here are a few guidelines:

1. Remember, a contract is only as good as the people signing it. If you don't think the facility is being honest with you, or you feel uncomfortable in any way about the contractual arrangements, don't sign them. Go back for clarification or go to another facility if they cannot or will not satisfy your questions about money terms or arrangements.

2. Whether you use your contract or theirs is not what is important. The important point is to know exactly what you are signing and make sure that *everything* you agreed upon is clearly written down—descriptions of things and services, time frames, costs, and people responsible. Never skip any fine print and never *assume* anything.

3. If the facility is not willing to exchange contracts with you in a very short time period following your negotiating session, or they will not commit themselves to a price or a reasonable range of prices with ceilings (upper price limits) included, then you should become very suspicious. Any facility that wants your business will show good faith by being willing to state all the details in writing.

4. Use terms in the contract that tie down prices, amounts of things, and time frames, such as "tax and gratuities included (or not included)"; "complete—no extras"; "to be delivered by, set up by, prepared by, available by, such-and-such a date" (you may even want to include the time of day).

5. Be flexible in your thinking. Be exacting and firm in your arrangements and contract. But also keep in mind the fact that you may need to change the contract as time goes by. So may the facility. These contracts are bilateral, not unilateral, which means it's a two-way street.

chapter fifteen
PHOTOGRAPHER

You may say, "What do I need a photographer for?" Consider taking pictures of these events:

1. The announcement boards in the facility announcing your seminar (outside, in the lobby, and by your seminar room).
2. Participants checking in, socializing, interacting during the seminar and at the breaks, lunching.
3. Introduction of the speaker/trainer.
4. The seminar in action.
5. Your staff interacting.

Don't be afraid to have a photographer—or someone taking pictures at the seminar. It lends an air of "special occasion" to the event. And everyone loves to be part of an event.

What would you use photographs for?

- Action pictures in a brochure or announcement form are very effective. Remember the old saying, "One picture is worth a thousand words." When using pictures where people are recognizable, obtain a permission form from them to use the picture. Consult an attorney for the proper wording and procedure.
- Take pictures of the participants and post them on display boards during the actual seminar. The participants will gather around during breaks;

the pictures create enthusiasm and excitement. Everyone likes to see pictures of themselves. They moan and groan and say, "Oh, I look awful!" But they can't resist looking anyway. Taking a person's picture is a way of saying "You are important," and don't we all like to feel important?

- A pictorial history of a seminar or series of seminars is a fun project; it creates enthusiasm among the staff. Everyone can pore over the pictures after the seminar and recall special things that happened.

- As a follow-up surprise, send pictures of the participants to them. It is a great public relations idea. How many times have you received a picture of yourself at a seminar? Probably never! Try it and watch the reaction.

If your company is putting on the seminar, you may have someone in-house who could do the job.

If you are conducting a public seminar, perhaps a friend could come along and take the pictures. Try renting a professional camera; it doesn't cost all that much and the results are worth the money.

If you can afford to hire a professional photographer, compare fees carefully. You will be surprised at the variation in shooting fees. Photographers specialize too, so hire one who has experience with this sort of photography.

chapter sixteen
HANDY DANDY SCOUT BOX

During the seminar you will need to have various items handy. Follow the scouts' motto: "Be prepared." As you begin the physical preparations for the seminar, start a list of the items for your Handy Dandy Scout Box. These are the everyday things you always seem to need, but never have with you. Here are a few to spur your imagination:

scissors
packing knife
masking tape
cellophane tape
paper clips—large and regular
stapler and staples
small hammer
small screwdriver
assortment of nails
measuring tape
Handi-wipes (clean all sorts of things besides people)
glue—regular and superhold types
chalk and eraser
pointer

extra audiovisual needs:
   light bulbs
   slide tray
   carousel tray
   splicing tape
   blank transparencies
typing white-out fluid
safety pins and straight pins
first-aid kit
sponge
spot-remover fluid
thread and needle
extra mailing labels
extra name tags
cash box and change
pushpins—thumbtacks

clear nail polish (mends all sorts of things)

cassette tape and recorder

batteries

extension cord, long

phone message pads

small camera, film, flash cubes, or flash attachment

throat lozenges (for speakers)

stopwatch

rubber bands

string or twine

extra plain white 8-1/2-by-11-inch paper

flashlight

Add your own special items to this list. Better to be overly prepared than to wish you had brought that one item you thought was unimportant.

Ask a Pro

Interview with:
Mr. Bob Radke
Manager, Education and Conferences, MEETING PLANNERS INTERNATIONAL
Middletown, Ohio

SHEILA: What advice would you give to someone new to the job of staging seminars?

BOB: I would suggest that someone new to the job of staging seminars acquire some basic texts on meeting-room environments. Then join a meeting planning organization, such as Meeting Planners International (MPI), or other types of organizations to get to know the people who are in the planning profession. You start reading a little bit, you talk a little bit here and there, you meet people and learn from their experience and your own experiences. That's how most of us got started in this business. There's an old statement that says, "The smart person learns from experience, the wise person learns from other people's experience."

In addition, try to remember what was good and what was bad about previous seminars that you have attended to determine what makes a successful seminar.

SHEILA: Is there a single most important item in staging a seminar?

BOB: I think the most important item is picking out a location that is easy to get to, has a good learning atmosphere, and is equipped to handle all your needs. That encompasses all of the audiovisual things that you may require on site.

SHEILA: In staging seminars, what do you think is the most common mistake?

BOB: I think the most common mistake is not getting a true reading of audience profile. Your seminar speaker/trainer needs to gear the material to the level of your audience. Also, there's an article I would suggest your readers send for from Bill Publication's "Successful Meetings" series, entitled "Are Your Troops Meeting—Prepared? Here Are 10 Steps That Will Make Your Meetings More Meaningful for Attendees," authored by Arthur R. Pell. In this article there are ten points that are basically designed to help the seminar planner or leader inform prospective seminar participants of what they should or should not do to get the most out of that meeting or seminar. It's a two-page article. It is the most helpful I have ever seen in assisting a participant to get the most out of a seminar. These two things are what many people forget when planning or conducting a seminar.

SHEILA: Do you have a final comment?

BOB: A final comment would be, know your market, price your seminar realistically, promote it consistently, and build a credible reputation; do these four things and you will insure the success of your seminar.

chapter seventeen
FOOD AND REFRESHMENTS

During the on-site tour you need to do the advance work on the food or refreshments you will serve during the seminar. You can discuss this with the sales department of the facility; however, it is best to go directly to the catering department whenever possible.

The facilities you will tour and eventually use are always eager to please when it comes to this service. They make more profit on food and beverage service than on the rental of seminar rooms.

As you review their menu, ask if there is a group being served during your tour. If there is, perhaps you can taste a sample of their refreshments or meal. This can give you a good idea of what your seminar will have in store for the participants.

It is best not to order exotic items. Don't order things because you prefer them. The facility will be able to tell you what is a neutral item preferred by most people. (They keep records of which dishes are received well and those that are not.)

As you discuss costs and guarantees for food and beverage service, remember to estimate your attendance and then order 10 percent less. Two things will happen. First, a 10 percent average no-show in attendance is a good figure to begin with. After you have had a few seminars, your figures on attendance will tell you if the 10 percent is too high or too low. The second thing that happens is that most facilities never prepare exactly the amount you order. They have a figure they build in to their preparations for extra servings in case you need them. Even though they require you to tell them exactly how many partici- pants you plan to have in attendance, they can adjust to a degree of 10 percent.

In your discussion, find out where the food or beverages will be prepared and who will serve them. If you are having a hot meal and the preparation center is in another building, to then be transported to your room, find out how it will be transported. You want to insure that the meals will remain hot or cold depending on how they start out from the kitchen.

Will there be facility staff to assist at a refreshment break? Or will the participants be helping themselves from a table or area near the seminar room? Either way is fine, you just need to know what's what.

If you are having a large group (over one hundred people) at the seminar and you will be serving coffee from urns, it can take a long time to let participants help themselves. It may be faster to have a facility person pour the coffee and hand it out.

Make sure the facility will be using coffee cups and saucers and real glasses rather than plastic or paper products. It is unprofessional to use the latter. If the facility won't or can't provide real dishes and glassware, perhaps you should take a second, very close look at this location. Can it really provide the overall comfort and professional image you want to project? Some facilities will moan and groan, but you should insist on having it done properly.

Now let's look at the times to have food and refreshments served, and a few tips to consider.

MORNING EYE-OPENER

It is always a good idea to provide coffee, tea, and Sanka for a morning eye-opener before a seminar begins. The participants will appreciate it, and you will have a much more awake group of people. You may even want to have fruit juice and/or sweet rolls. Your budget will determine whether this is feasible. If not, you can make them available at a low cost to the participants.

MORNING REFRESHMENT BREAK

During your morning refreshment break you will probably want to serve the same type beverages as in the eye-opener. Ask the facility how they charge for coffee. Some charge by the cup, others by the urn or pot. There can be a great difference in price. Also ask if they include tea and Sanka in the coffee price, or will you have to pay extra for these? Some facilities include these in the overall coffee prices.

LUNCHEON BREAK

Consider having a buffet luncheon. This can be a very nice change of pace. It may not be less expensive than a luncheon entree, but cost is not always the only determining factor.

Regardless of what you choose to serve, make it light. It is very difficult to keep people's attention in the afternoon when they have had a heavy, filling lunch.

It is not a good idea to serve alcoholic beverages at any time, particularly not at lunchtime.

AFTERNOON REFRESHMENT BREAK

At some point in the afternoon you will need to take a break. There are facilities that offer some very nice alternatives in place of the old standby coffee and soft drinks. Fruit juice, yogurt, fresh fruit, and milk are being added to the old standards. You will find that offering this sort of variety will be very well received by your participants.

If you plan to serve fruit juice, ask for frozen rather than fresh (unless your budget can afford fresh juice). There is an enormous price difference between these two.

Here is an idea that can save money. When you order fruit juice, don't have it brought out in pitchers. People tend to take a glass and fill it with juice, then never finish it. Have the facility pour the juice in glasses half filled with ice, and then bring them out to be served. The juice will be nice and cold, and there will be enough juice in each glass to refresh the participants. Another money-saving idea is in regard to soft drinks. Facilities will charge you by the can or bottle. Find out what size cans and bottles they use. If they are the regular twelve-ounce cans, that is fine—just make sure they are well chilled. If the can size is larger than twelve ounces, you can have them do the same thing I suggested with the fruit juice: prepour. You will be surprised how many people will pick up one of those large-size cans or bottles and never finish drinking it. You will see your refreshment budget sitting around in half-finished cans and bottles.

The idea of an afternoon break is to give people a physical and mental break. You want to provide a food or drink that will bring their blood-sugar level up. Most people have low blood sugar in the mid- to late afternoon, which of course affects their ability to learn and pay attention. One of the alternatives to coffee and soft drinks will be a healthy, welcome change.

DINNER SERVICE

If your seminar will last longer than one day, you need to consider whether you will serve dinner. It is a good way to control the time involved in the evening meal and the level of alcohol consumed. An evening meal can and should be more substantial than the luncheon menu. Again, it is not a good idea to serve alcoholic beverages. You don't need hangovers in the morning session.

BEFORE-BED SNACKS

If your seminar will continue into the evening or if you are at a location where participants will be together after dinner, it is a very nice touch to have a before-bed snack. Keep it light and healthful—no caffeine.

For any of these food and refreshment services, make very careful note in your contractual arrangements with the facility:

- What is to be served and what time the service is to begin and end?
- Where is the service to take place and who will be serving?
- What number of guarantees will you be billed for and what are the arrangements for payment?

Be sure these questions are clearly answered—it will make your job and the facility's job a lot easier.

Always check the prices for any food or beverage service very carefully. Get a fixed price quote from the facility. You can't afford to plan a seminar and then find out on the day it takes place that the prices have gone up.

Food and beverage service is a very important part of your seminar. It can also be the most costly. Use your checklists, and tend carefully to details.

chapter eighteen
FIRE PROTECTION

As I was researching some material to include in this section I found the following excellent information. It is from the National Fire Protection Association. They have been kind enough to allow me to reprint this article in its entirety.

The National Fire Protection Association conducts seminars and trains meeting planners on fire safety. You may contact them for further information at:

National Fire Protection Association
Batterymarch Park
Quincy, MA 02269

INFORMATION ON HOTEL AND MOTEL FIRESAFETY FOR MEETING PLANNERS

A meeting planner's primary responsibility is to make certain that the attendees are comfortable, safe, and secure. The safety aspect includes firesafety, and the meeting planner's responsibility in that area is continuous. Responsibility for firesafety begins with the selection of the facility long before the meeting convenes and lasts until the attendees have left. The National Fire Protection Association has published the following information to help meeting planners discharge that responsibility:

Firesafety in hotels involves the application of some fundamentals of fire protection to create a life safety "system." While the "system" may vary from building to building, the fundamentals remain the same. Variations occur only in the methods used to apply the fundamentals to attain a reasonable level of life safety from fire. Hotels are categorized under at least two separate occupancy classes — residential and assembly — and the life safety system for the two classes will be different.

A meeting planner cannot be expected to be sufficiently knowledgeable in the science of fire prevention and protection to study and evaluate the life safety "system" of a hotel. However, if the planner is familiar with some fundamentals, he or she will be able to question the hotel manager regarding the hotel's firesafety features.

The planner should consider the following five fundamentals:

- *Detection and Notification.* The provisions made for detecting the occurrence of a fire, and the method by which the attendees will be alerted that this is a fire emergency.

- *Means of Egress.* The number and adequacy of the routes taken by attendees to reach exits, the conditions of the exits, and the paths from the termination of the exits to reach a safe place outside.

- *Time to Reach an Exit.* The features of building construction (floors, walls, etc.) that com-

partment the building to prevent fire spread — finishes on walls and ceilings that do not spread fire, and mechanical services (air conditioning) that do not spread heat and smoke before attendees have time to reach exits.

- *Extinguishment.* The provisions made for extinguishing a fire either manually or automatically.

- *Employee Training.* The presence of a training program for employees on how to prevent fire and what to do in a fire emergency, including a written emergency fire plan.

Firesafety codes and standards vary from jurisdiction to jurisdiction, as do the levels of enforcement and compliance.

It would be impractical for a meeting planner to inspect a hotel or meeting facility and be confident that he or she has covered all the details and provisions that constitute a firesafe building. Only qualified fire protection specialists can carry out such a thorough inspection.

There are certain aspects of building firesafety that the meeting planner can personally ascertain, and other aspects where the planner must rely on others.

The following lists cover items on which information should be obtained from others, and also some of the items that the meeting planner can look for during a preselection visit.

It may well be that not each and every one of the items identified in the lists will be in the affirmative. The meeting planner will then have to consider whether there are compensatory factors, and in this professional advice should be sought.

In all cases where the meeting planner is in doubt about firesafety requirements, he or she should seek expert opinion from fire protection officials. Sources for such opinion are state and local fire officials, or private consulting fire protection engineers. In some instances, state and local fire officials are not permitted to express opinions on a specific building, but they can be expected to inform you of the codes and standards that are required to be met in their jurisdiction.

However, the information required should first be sought from the management of the hotel or meeting facility. The following basic questions should be asked:

- Is the facility subject to any fire or safety regulations or laws?

- If the answer to above is yes, what codes or standards are applied to the facility under such regulations or laws?

- If the answer is no, what firesafety codes or standards are applied by the hotel voluntarily?

- Is the facility in compliance with the fire codes and standards applied?

- Has the facility been inspected recently for compliance by the local fire marshal or equivalent official of the jurisdiction in which it is located?

- Are there any violations outstanding or uncorrected at the time of this inquiry?

- If violations are outstanding or uncorrected, will they be eliminated by the date that the meeting planner wants to use the facilities?

- Does the facility have an established, operating emergency procedure in case of fire?

- Are all members of the staff trained and drilled regularly in emergency procedure? (NFPA recommends monthly drills.)

- Does the emergency procedure include requirements that:
  - All reports of the fire are to be immediately reported to the public fire department?

- All reports of fire are to be immediately responded to by staff?

- Occupants at risk are to be alerted promptly of a fire?

- The fire alarm system is to be tested at least monthly or as required by local law, and a report submitted to management on the conditions found when the alarm was tested?

- When provided, detection and extinguishing systems are to be maintained and tested regularly?

- Is a senior management official responsible for supervision of, and accountable for, the emergency procedure?

- Has the staff been instructed in the following:

  - To report fires immediately, and how to do so?

  - How to recognize and report apparent fire hazards?

  - How to recognize and report malfunctions to the alarm systems, exit and emergency lighting, door closing devices, and fire equipment, etc.?

  - To remove obstructions to exit ways, including carts, rollaway beds, food service trays, laundry bags, etc.?

- Is the telephone switchboard operated 24 hours a day?

- Have arrangements been made with the local fire department for cooperative action in the event of a fire?

The responses to these questions should give the planner an indication of the status of the facility in relation to local codes and some basic requirements for firesafety. The planner should verify any point on which the response does not seem to be satisfactory. This approach, that of being assured in effect that the facility is firesafe, relies on two presumptions: one, that the local fire codes are adequate and are properly enforced; and two, that the facility's management is prepared to provide the information suggested. It is recommended that the responses be

131

reviewed with the safety director of the meeting planner's organization or by an independent professional fire protection specialist.

PRESELECTION SITE VISIT

Meeting planners can check the following items for themselves, in addition to obtaining the information from the facility management:

- That there is a fire alarm system to alert the attendees of a fire.

- That exit doors and routes to them are indicated by illuminated "exit" sign.

- That there is emergency lighting for the exit ways and exit stairs.

- That there are no obstructions in corridors, exit doorways, exit stairs, and other routes that constitute exit ways for occupants.

- That exit doors are not locked or secured in any way that would prevent ready use of the door.

- That doors to exit stairs close and latch automatically after use and remain properly closed.

- That instructions are prominently displayed in each attendee's room, giving details of the fire alarm signal and indicating locations of the nearest exits.

- That attendee's room doors are self-closing and do not have transoms or louvres that might permit penetration of smoke into the room.

- That there is a sign in each elevator lobby station that "elevators are not to be used during a fire."

- That there are signs posted at the principal entrance to meeting and facility rooms specifying maximum number of occupants.

- That meeting rooms have sufficient exits to allow the number of occupants to leave readily, based on the following ratio:

    more than 1,000 — 4 exits
    300-1,000 — 3 exits
    50-300 — 2 exits

- That the provided exits are remote from each other so that occupants are able to use alternatives if one exit becomes unusable in an emergency.

- That the corridors, stairways, and aisles are free of temporary or permanent storage including laundry, chairs, tables, room service trays and trash, etc.

- That any folding partitions or air walls are arranged so as not to obstruct access to required exits.

- That exhibit areas are provided with automatic extinguishing systems (sprinklers), and if not, alternative arrangements and provisions are provided to compensate for lack of such sprinkler protection.

- That there are adequate services and facilities available in the exhibit areas for removal of packing and other combustible materials before the exhibit opens, and that no such materials are allowed to accumulate on the premises during the exhibition.

- That the layout of booths, stands, and exhibits will not impede or block exits and exit routes.

- That a fire watch is maintained in exhibit areas when setting up the exhibit, during the exhibit, and during exhibit breakdown to spot fire hazards and detect fires, and that the fire department is to be called if an emergency occurs.

- That there be a number of approved receptacles for the disposal of smoking material in meeting rooms and exhibit facilities.

- That local codes and ordinances are observed regarding the use of flammable and combustible materials as a part of the meeting or exhibition.

AT THE MEETING

The meeting planner should arrange for the following:

- That preconference meetings with meeting facilities staff include a discussion of fire-safety procedures.

- That chairs, platforms, head tables, screens, and projectors are arranged so that they do not block aisles or exits.

- That there are no more than 14 seats between aisles or no more than 7 seats between a wall and an aisle, and that there are aisles and cross aisles provided for *direct* access to exits.

- That in meeting rooms seating more than 200 people, seats are fastened to the floor or fastened to each other.

- That exits are unlocked and free and clear of any obstructions.

- That attendees in meeting rooms are advised of exit locations at the start of the meeting.

- That attendees are provided with literature and information on what they should be prepared for in the event of a fire.*

- That the planner's staff and presiding officers have instructions on action to take and announcements to make to the attendees if a fire emergency should occur, and that those instructions are coordinated with the hotel Fire Emergency Plan.

- That there is staff assigned to all of the tasks indicated previously under the title, "At The Meeting."

*A leaflet suitable for insertion in travel or registration envelopes is available from NFPA.

This publication is not intended to be a complete discussion of, or standard for, all firesafety problems involving hotels, motels, or meeting planning. Local codes and ordinances, as well as the actions of individuals, all affect the safety of organizations or persons using such facilities.

NFPA recommends that the provisions of NFPA standard 101 — 1981, the *Life Safety Code®*, be followed in all such facilities. However, this *Code* may not have been adopted by local jurisdictions, and in such cases, local codes or ordinances will prevail.

The advice contained in this document does not constitute an NFPA standard; it is intended only to assist meeting planners in fulfilling their responsibility. Reference should be made to NFPA codes and standards for the official policy of the Association in respect to firesafety requirements.

®Reg. TM: The National Fire Protection Association, Inc.

chapter nineteen

MISCELLANEOUS

PERMITS AND LICENSING

If you will be conducting your seminar in an area, city, or state that is unfamiliar to you, it is a good idea to contact the local governing agencies. Find out if they have any special licensing or permit regulations. For example:

1. Do you need a license or permit to use the seminar facility?
2. Is the parking area open twenty-four hours a day? Do you need permits to use it or keep it open?

I was in the Midwest conducting a seminar as part of a large conference, which consisted of several seminars throughout the day and into the evening. The last seminar concluded at 10 P.M. We all walked out out of the conference center to go back to our hotels. To our amazement, the local police were having all the guests' cars towed away.

We finally found out that the small parking area next to the conference center was not really a parking lot. There was a tiny No Trespassing sign lying on the ground, which had fallen off a post. No one had seen it! It seemed like a convenient place to park, and the townspeople parked there too. As the police towed the cars away, we tried to discuss this with them. To no avail! That was the night the police decided to enforce the tow-away law. What a mess! It pays to be very aware of the areas adjoining your seminar facility. When taking your on-site tour, look out for innocent-looking parking areas.

3. If you will be serving any liquor during the seminar breaks, lunch, or dinner, do you need a license? What are the local regulations?

INTERNAL REVENUE SERVICE

If you have not done so yet, find out if your seminar is deductible as a training expense. Check with the IRS for its rulings. Then pass the information along to the participants. It may make a difference to someone's budget and decision to attend.

TIPPING—"TO INSURE PROMPTNESS"

The term *tip* is the abbreviation for "to insure promptness." Most people leave a tip or gratuity *after* the event or service. Try turning that around and see what happens. People respond positively to a vote of confidence before the fact. You may think that if you give someone a tip before the service rather than afterward, they will not do as good a job. It seems to work in just the opposite way.

I was planning a series of evening seminars in a hotel, so I contacted the head of the sales department and went in for our first meeting. After a very productive hour of exchanging information and strategy planning, I left and went to a local florist. I had them send a beautiful hanging plant to her office along with a handwritten thank-you note from me. I thanked her for her time and efforts on my behalf. I said what a pleasure it was going to be working with her in the coming months.

The evening of the first seminar I arrived early to make sure all the details were taken care of, and there she was, overseeing the details herself (long after the usual end of her working day). She continued to be there before each subsequent seminar. The service was impeccable. Our relationship got off to a super start and remained that way through the entire series of seminars. I indeed received "promptness."

I know a gentleman who frequents a restaurant in Los Angeles. The first time he dined there, he was so impressed that he knew he would return often. Upon arrival the second time he tipped the parking attendant, doorman, maître d'hôtel, head waiter, waiter, and wine

steward—*in advance.* Dining with him at that restaurant is an unbeliev-
able experience. He and his guests are treated like royalty. He tips in
advance.

In dealing with anyone you would eventually reward in relation
to their work for your seminar, consider insuring promptness and tip in
advance. It works wonders.

Ask a Pro

Interview with:
Mr. Tommy Hopkins
President, CHAMPIONS UNLIMITED
Scottsdale, Arizona

SHEILA: What advice would you give to someone new to the job of staging
          seminars?
TOMMY: I would say have a very detailed checklist prior to the program. Find
          out who at the locations is going to be in charge of all the details.
          Meet that person in the morning to be sure that everything is done
          exactly as you want it. Know who will be there during the seminar
          to be sure that everything goes well. I have a detailed checklist that
          goes out thirty days in advance, and I have constant communication
          with that person before the seminar.
SHEILA: Is there a single most important item in staging a seminar?
TOMMY: There is not one single most important factor. The three factors that
          I consider most important are a good microphone, good air-
          conditioning system, and room setup. I personally have a ramp that
          goes out thirty to forty feet into the room so that there is a centergy
          (a feeling of oneness, closeness) between me and the audience. If
          these three things aren't working, you are going to have a hard time
          keeping the audience interested.
SHEILA: In staging seminars, what do you think is the most common mis-
          take?
TOMMY: I think the most common problem is that people arrive to do a
          seminar and they haven't made arrangements for all of the contin-
          gencies, all of the things that can go wrong, in advance. I have two
          people who go in advance of my seminars the day before and make
          sure that everything is just right so that when I walk on the stage,
          it's perfect and all set to go. I have no problems.
SHEILA: Do you have a final comment?
TOMMY: Sheila, I want to thank you for writing this book for our industry. I
          think it's fantastic!

chapter twenty
SHIPPING SUPPLIES AND MATERIALS

If you will be transporting equipment or materials to and from the seminar location either before, during, or after the seminar, check with the facility on how to handle these arrangements. Does the facility have a specific department for shipping and receiving? If so, what hours are they open? Who is in charge?

If there is not a specific department or person in charge, to whom should the materials be shipped? What name and/or department should they be sent to the attention of? What specific arrangements need to be made in advance? Get names, addresses, department number, phone number, telephone extension, etc., of people who will receive these materials.

To ship materials or supplies in advance of the seminar date, these ideas will make the job easier:

1. If the items you are shipping have been sent to you in a box or carton:
    A. Check to see that they are properly padded. Packing for a journey across town is not sufficient for a journey across the state or country.
    B. If the box or carton is in good condition and you plan to send the items on to the seminar, reinforce the outside with heavy-duty packing tape. The best kind to use is one that has plastic fibers through it. It won't come off in wet weather and is practically impervious to bumps and scratches.

2. If you must pack the items yourself, spend the extra money and purchase heavy-duty cartons. The kind that professional movers use are best. Then reinforce the outside with the same type of tape mentioned above.

3. When you decide the mode of transportation you will use, call and ask for any suggestions or requirements that the carrier may have for preparing the boxes for shipment.

4. If your supplies are fragile, ask the shipping company to send you their labels for special handling instructions.

5. Think ahead to the return trip of the supplies and/or materials. Put a pair of scissors and packing tape and return labels into one of the boxes, then seal and send. When you open it, the items for the return trip are all there. Even though you have a Handy Dandy Scout Box with you, the shipping may not occur at a time or place when you can use those supplies.

LABELS

1. When you take the supplies with you by car, train, or airplane, mark them with a label that reads:

THIS BOX ACCOMPANIES: Your name, company name, address, phone number

> TO: Name of seminar facility
> Street address
> City, state, ZIP code
> Telephone number
> Date of seminar: Include the time of day

> FOR: Seminar entitled (your seminar title)
> Seminar location (name of room seminar is in)
> Contents of box

Never take it for granted that you and your supplies will arrive at the same time or at the same location, even when you take them with you. Believe it or not, I once drove to a seminar location, pulled up in front of the hotel, unloaded my box of supplies, parked the car and came back to pick up the supply box and go to the seminar room. Surprise—the box was gone! A helpful bellman had taken it to another seminar in the same facility. It took one hour to find my supply box because I had not labeled it.

2. When shipping ahead to the seminar, mark each box with:
   A. Whatever the shipping firm requires for labels or special handling.
   B. Then add your own label with the following information:
      "From" information:
      > Your name, title, company name, street address, city, state, ZIP code, and telephone number.
      >
      > The date you shipped the package or gave it to the carrier. Include the time of day, when possible.

      "To" information:
      > Seminar facility name, street address, city, state, ZIP code.
      >
      > Attention: name of contact person who will sign for box at the facility, their telephone number and/or extension.
      >
      > Date the box is expected to arrive
      >
      > If there is no one to act as contact person to receive your materials, write Hold for the arrival of (Your name and name of company)
      > On (Date of your arrival)
      >
      > Seminar information:
      > For:
      > Seminar room (Name and location)
      > Seminar date and time
      > Contents of box

3. If your supplies are to be shipped to one destination, such as an airport, and a ground carrier is to pick them up and deliver them to the seminar location, your label should include that information. For example:
   > Shipped by:
   > Arrival date expected
   > Who will pick it up
   > Date of pickup

4. To make sure you have proof of proper labeling, type or mark your labels on large gum-backed labels, or use plain white paper and tape it to the box. Make a duplicate to keep on file in case something happens to the box and you must trace its location.

   You may want to take the duplicate with you to the seminar for the same reason, or to prove you shipped it properly, or to enable someone searching for it to recognize your label.

5. Even if you use gummed labels, take clear packing tape and completely cover the face of the label. Have the tape extend over the label to the box itself. Printing on labels has been known to run or fade in wet weather. Labels have also been cut in half or pulled off because of a loose edge. Taping insures their permanence.

LAND VERSUS AIR

When deciding which mode of transportation you wish to use for shipping your supplies and materials, there are time and cost decisions to be made.

1. Shipping by land usually costs less, but takes longer.

2. If you are shipping across state lines, many carriers are not able to go into another state, so they have arrangements by which other carriers pick up the cargo at the border and take it from there. When you call the ground carrier you intend to use, ask if this is the case. If it is, get the name, address, and telephone number of the carrier that will be responsible at the final destination. The same holds true for some air carriers—they may not fly directly to your seminar location. They may pass cargo onto another line.

3. Are your supplies being delivered to a central location from which a local ground service will deliver them to the seminar facility? If so, follow the who, what, when, where method in your inquiries.

4. If you have very special shipping requirements, you may need to find a specialist to do the job. Most common carriers I have used try to handle all the various needs, but sometimes it is not possible. Always tell them exactly what you need. They don't want to mishandle your shipment and will tell you if they can't handle a very special job.

5. Always compare all costs in shipping before deciding whether to use ground or air service. Don't take someone else's word for it. At one point in my career I was shipping one large box ahead of me to each seminar. I heard from a speaker that it was best to ship the box a certain way, with a certain company. Shortly after I had begun using the suggested method of shipping I was called on to do a last-minute seminar, and I did not have time to ship ahead by ground transport. I rushed to the airport with my supply box, expecting to pay an air freight charge. When I checked in I had one suitcase and my box of supplies. The counter person picked both up, weighed them, tagged them, and off they went in the luggage compartment of the plane. I was so surprised! I found that I was allowed two pieces of luggage on most every flight, and that my box of supplies could be counted as one of those pieces of luggage. I have saved incredible amounts of time and money doing it this way. I should have checked my options much earlier.

6. Services that provide overnight delivery are excellent when you need emergency shipping service. Research their names, rates, specifications, and telephone numbers, as well as what cities they deliver to. Keep this information handy—you never know when you may need it. Take it with you when you go to the seminar in case you must call home and

have something sent that you've forgotten. The fees are high in comparison to regular shipping, but when you need the service, you will be happy to pay the price.

7. Weather and season may play a part in your shipping decisions. In the dead of winter it may be more effective to ship by air. The cost will be more, but the problems that otherwise could accrue are obvious. Upon occasion, it has taken me as long as four weeks to ship by truck from one coast to the other in winter.

8. I'd like to say that all airlines are super-careful and try to take very good care of your shipment, whether shipped in advance or taken on the flight with you. Unfortunately, some really miss the boat, so to speak.

I was in a major airport awaiting a flight. As I stood in the waiting area, looking out the window, I noticed that the man next to me was very upset. After a few moments his distress was so extreme I asked if he were ill and was there something I could do for him.

He just pointed out the window at the baggage handlers, who were unloading an airplane. He moaned and said, "Those boxes are mine!" I looked again and saw that the baggage handler who was standing at the door of the airplane baggage area had an arm the U.S. Olympic shot put team should know about. He was taking this man's boxes (which were clearly marked Fragile), lifting them to his shoulder and tossing them, shot-put style, to the man on the ground, who in turn tossed them onto the baggage cart. The man told me he was on his way to a trade show for his industry, and those boxes were filled with fine crystal wine glasses. Even with the careful packing he described to me it didn't take much imagination to picture the present condition of those wineglasses.

This is not an indictment of all air carriers, but if you have special needs, such as that man did, you should communicate them directly to the carrier's ground crews.

chapter twenty-one
PRINTING

Printed matter for a seminar, whether it is preseminar announcements or the seminar handout material, probably means something different to each person reading this book. A rule for everyone is, "Remember, everything always takes longer than you plan."

Have one staff person in charge of all printing. This is not an area you want groups of people working on. Too many cooks spoil the soup. When deciding whether you wish to use a printer to prepare part or all of your printed material, be sure to get out your Shopping List Questionnaire and talk to as many suppliers as possible, suppliers such as wholesale paper companies, typesetters, and printers.

Some of the worst budget overruns are in printing costs. A good list of well-reasoned questions will go a long way in preventing these overruns in your seminar budget.

Here are some questions to ask yourself:

1. Do you want to use a printer to do the whole job?
2. Do you want to have a typesetter prepare the material and then make the copies yourself?
3. Will you save money and time by using a printer who can order the paper, do the typesetting and printing? Or do you need a separate typesetter and printer?
4. Can you buy paper stock wholesale? In relation to time, does this really save money?

5. Will a "quick print" shop be able to do the job for you, compared to a regular printer?
6. Are your supplier charges equal to their ability? Have you seen samples of their work?
7. When deciding if you want to prepare your own materials, do you have available or can you rent or buy:
   A. The kind of typewriter that can adjust margins and/or type so the result looks typeset?
   B. The equipment that can print in various sizes and styles of type? The words come out on a gummed tape that you can set on a piece of paper to design your own materials.
   C. Do you have access to materials that printers use for standard drawings, cartoon characters, etc.?

When using a typesetter and/or printer, allow plenty of time to proof all of the work. No matter how careful a printing supplier is, the margin for error is great. Make sure that the printing is exactly as you want it before it goes to press. Have them issue a "blue line." This is a proof sheet of what your finished work will look like.

In dealing with the printer or printing supplier, follow the rule of having a written contract or agreement with them. No matter how large or small your order, have a written estimate or bid in advance of your decision to order whatever it is you need. Whenever you make a change and add or subtract from the original agreement, be sure to put it in writing and send it to the printer for initialing.

If you are new to the job of seminar planning, print 10 percent more materials than you anticipate needing. You always want to be sure to have extras for last-minute needs. After some experience, you will arrive at a percentage of extra printing best suited for your seminar.

If you are planning your first public seminar, don't print thousands of anything when you are only going to need a few hundred. People will advise you on the savings when you print large amounts. The problem you encounter is that you will probably change the material several times before you are totally pleased with the content and/or use. If you have thousands of the thing on hand, you will feel guilty about throwing them away and starting over, even when you aren't happy with them.

In closing this section on printing, I want to again warn you to

avoid cost-overrun problems by allowing more time than you think you
need for your printed matter.

Ask a Pro

Interview with:
Ms. Deborah K. Gaffney
Director of Conference Management, DIRECT SELLING ASSOCIATION
Washington, D.C.

SHEILA: What advice would you give to someone new to the job of staging
seminars?

DEBORAH: Get help from people with experience! Utilize all the resources at
your disposal. Find out who's accomplished a task you're suddenly
faced with. Ask them how they did it; why it worked, or didn't.
Leave your mind wide open to alternatives—there is no "right" way
to achieve the result you're after. Lean heavily on the advice of
those whose business it is to carry out elements of your seminar:
artists, printers, convention service managers, catering managers,
a/v technicians, etcetera. They've all seen more water flow under
the bridge than you—learn from their experience.

SHEILA: Is there a single most important item in staging a seminar?

DEBORAH: Put one person in charge—and make sure everyone knows who he
or she is. Think of it as analagous to the captain of a ship: Each of his
officers reports to him on the various activities for which he is
responsible; the captain weighs the alternatives, makes his decisions, and gives the orders. This is especially important for smooth
operations during the seminar itself. All information should flow
through this individual.

SHEILA: In staging seminars, what do you think is the most common
mistake?

DEBORAH: Two most common mistakes, to which I give equal weight, are: not
understanding your audience, and not understanding your
finances.

Often a planner becomes so bogged down in details, he/she
loses sight of "Who is the seminar for, anyway?" Always step back
and try to put yourself in the attendees' shoes. If *you* were attending
this seminar, what would *you* want to get out of it? What information would *you* need to insure a worthwhile expenditure of your
valuable time and/or money?

Four little words that many planners never utter frequently
enough: "How much is it?" I believe that is self-explanatory!

SHEILA: Do you have a final comment?

DEBORAH: Organize thyself! Set up foolproof systems that allow you to put your hands on any piece of information at any time, and that tell you when deadlines are coming up. Developing these systems takes time—and trial and error. After each meeting you will have at least one detail you now know should be considered or attended to prior to the meeting. Incorporate it into the system! Finalize as many details as you possibly can prior to your meeting. Enough last-minute crises will occur without having to worry about ones that could have been solved weeks ago.

part three
COMMUNICATIONS WITH PARTICIPANTS

chapter twenty-two
TIME FRAMES

As you approach the subject of communicating with the seminar participants, step back and view the process from their position. Think in terms of what you would want to know or receive from the sponsor of a seminar you were planning to attend. What information would make you comfortable about attending? What would give you the impression of professionalism about the sponsor of the seminar?

These are the ideas to keep in mind as you develop your checklist, flow chart, and delegation of tasks for communication with participants.

There are four time frames to be aware of in the participants' communication process. Let's take each of these four time frames and enumerate some items to include in your checklist and flow charts.

"ADVANCE" COMMUNICATION
TIME FRAME

As soon as you have all of your basic information as to seminar location, time and date, facility, travel information, costs, etc., you can start the communication process with your participants.

If you are conducting a public seminar, your marketing program would, of course, include these ideas and information.

If you are conducting a seminar within your own group (as opposed to marketing it to the general public), these ideas and information are also for you.

Keep in mind that in the advance time frame communications you want to transmit only the major items of concern. Save the details—such as facility maps and dress code—for the next (close-in) communication time frame.

Items to cover in advance communications:

Questionnaire

This is your opportunity to ask all the questions you need answered for a successful seminar (in relationship to the participant). Such questions can include:

1. Anything you want to know that is pertinent to the subject matter and material being presented. Included in this questionnaire could be instructions that participants must follow in preparation to attend the seminar, e.g., books or papers to read, research, material to gather.
2. Experience or information on other seminars attended.
3. Expectations about you and/or your seminar.

Promotional Material

Any promotional material—such as brochures, publicity items, and seminar outlines—should be included.

Participants' Travel Checklist

This checklist, found in Section II, Chapter 7, should be sent to all participants at this time.

Registration and Billing

A full explanation of your registration and billing process should be included. A further explanation of these will follow in this section. Just remember—keep it simple, or you will find yourself bogged down in a mess you won't believe.

"CLOSE-IN" COMMUNICATION
TIME FRAME

A definition of what "close-in" means is not possible. Your own time frames will define this for you. For example, if you are planning a seminar in your own area and there is no need for extended travel or overnight accommodation confirmations, two to three weeks is probably a workable time frame for "close-in" communications. If, however, you are planning a seminar where the participants must travel great distances and make complicated reservations for hotel rooms, cars, and so forth, two or more months may be appropriate.

Just make sure you allow enough time between the advance communication time frame and the close-in time frame to exchange and relate all the appropriate information that you and your participants will need. The close-in time frame communications may have several steps. Give yourself plenty of time between the close-in and the "day of" time frame. There may be changes, cancellations, reconfirmations, or any number of things that simply cannot be taken care of in a single close-in communication.

Here then are some items to begin your close-in communication list:

1. A confirmation form showing registration and billing details.
2. Transportation information and confirmations.
    As I have said before, try not to become directly involved in the handling of travel or overnight accommodations unless they are included as part of your seminar costs.
    Include any helpful information you have, such as directions and travel maps, facility layout maps, directions to your seminar room or other building locators, the names of your staff or facility staff to contact for assistance.
3. If there is need for overnight accommodations, include the details. If the participants are handling this themselves and you are simply helping people find roommates, etc., this is the time to share this information.
4. Include a list of city services and emergency services that are appropriate for your seminar location, such as:
    Tow trucks (for snowy winter locations)
    Police—address and telephone number
    State highway patrol or troopers—address and telephone number
    Fire department

Convention and Visitors' Bureau

Tourists' information offices

List of special events in the area

5. If there are any special permits or licenses necessary, include them or information about them. For example, will your participants need a sticker or pass to park their car in a location near the seminar? If so, include it or tell them how to obtain it.

6. Dietary or disabled needs. Do they have any? What can you do to make their seminar experience more pleasant and meaningful? Ask these questions and provide this information.

7. Dress code—is there any? If you are planning to use a resort area, list what clothing would be most appropriate. If you are planning to use a seminar room setup that includes floor or ground sitting, indicate this. If the participants will dine out, is a coat and tie required? If so, mention this. Make sure that you don't take for granted that people know what is appropriate or comfortable for your seminar location. Put them at ease.

8. If they are required to bring any special equipment or materials, make a very clear list. Let them use it as a checklist for themselves. Last but not least, give them an outline of the seminar. If this seminar is special and you don't plan to repeat it, give specific dates, times, seminar room locations, and subject. If you plan to repeat the seminar, a general outline can be used and reused. The outline should include:

Seminar title

Morning session

Refreshment break

Conclusion of morning session

Lunch break

Afternoon session

Refreshment break

Conclusion of afternoon session and/or conclusion of seminar

Evening or postseminar event

Along with this outline, furnish information about the speaker/trainer.

"DAY OF" COMMUNICATION
TIME FRAME

Here it is, the day (or the first day) of the seminar. The participants are due to arrive. What information do you need to impart to them about the seminar, the requirements for them as participants, or the arrangements you have made for their special needs and/or general comfort and convenience?

If you will keep this thought in mind, it will make your job a lot easier: People will forget to bring any or all of the helpful information and items listed in the previous part, "Close-In" Communications. It is not that they are thoughtless or unaware. Human nature being what it is just does not allow for such perfection.

Your participants can be rushed and forget things. They can lose things. I have heard every conceivable explanation as to why something was left at home or forgotten. There are two instances that stick in my mind. Once I was conducting a seminar for a group of high school students and they were required to bring a small confirmation form to the first session. One young man arrived with a long face. He did not have his confirmation. He explained that his toddler-aged brother liked the bright pink color of the confirmation form so much, he ate it.

The second one that comes to mind concerns a woman who arrived at a seminar with a registration form in hand that looked like it had gone through the war. She started to giggle when explaining why the form looked so sad. (It also had no writing on it, just blue ink sloshed all over it.) She said she had gone to her post office box to pick up the mail. The registration form was included in a packet of information she received from me. She was opening the mail as she walked down the street. As she passed the park, a gust of wind whipped the form from her hand and sent it skipping across the park lawn. She ran to retrieve it, and at just that moment the sprinkler system went on. Here she was, getting drenched by the water, when the form, also now wet and soggy, came to rest on the lawn. As she ran to retrieve the form, another big gust of wind blew across the lawn. Afraid the form might stray, she stomped on it to keep it from moving. She finally picked it up and ran out of the range of the sprinkler. By the time she got through her tale of woe about the condition of the water-stiffened, ink-sloshed, stomped-on form, we were all near tears of laughter. All sorts of things can happen to information you provide.

This list of "day-of" communications will include some items from the close-in list plus a few others.

1. Seminar outline and S/T information
2. Overnight accommodations and arrangements

3. List of city services and emergency numbers
4. Special tipping or gratuity information
5. Facility staff and your staff person's names to go to for assistance
6. Special dietary or disabled persons' information
7. Dress-code specifications
8. Lost and found arrangements
9. Message, board, or box arrangements
10. Facility map or layout
11. List of special local events
12. Seminar name tags, identification badges, and meal tickets
13. Seminar workbook, handout, or materials
14. Evaluation forms or follow-up information that participants will need or that you require (you may wish to distribute these at the *conclusion* of the seminar)

"FOLLOW-UP" COMMUNICATION TIME FRAME

Follow-up communications can include evaluation forms and/or response cards that are given out at the seminar conclusion, or this communication may consist of information that you transmit to participants at a later date. (Refer to Section V, Evaluation, Follow-up, and Debriefing.)

Now that you have the four time frames in mind, what specific needs do you or your participants have that can be handled in the communications process?

The more detailed your checklist becomes, the better chance you have of avoiding major problems and/or omissions. You will grow with experience. Your participants themselves will be invaluable in learning how and what to do for and with them in the seminar communication process.

chapter twenty-three
PRESEMINAR REGISTRATION: PAYMENT AND BILLING SYSTEMS

The most important thing to remember about your payment and/or billing system for preseminar registration is to keep it simple! People hate filling out forms. So if you can cut the process short, it is a major plus factor in your favor.

METHODS OF PAYMENT

If you are conducting a public seminar it is absolutely, positively crucial to have your seminar participants preregister and pay in advance. There are several reasons why this is true:

1. When the participants pay in advance, they *attend* the seminar. Without this financial and accompanying emotional commitment, they will rarely show up, even when they say they will (verbally or in writing). The key is financial commitment.

2. You need time to clear checks and charge-card registrations, so if there is a problem you can correct it before the seminar.

3. If you are serving refreshments or meals, you will be required to pay for them once you have committed to the number you'll expect to have in attendance, even if the participants fail to attend.

4. Have a cutoff date for registration. This does two things: One, it lets you know how many participants to expect; and two, it creates an impending

event or feeling of urgency. (Remember when I said that anyone considering marketing or conducting public seminars should take a basic sales course?) This term *impending event* is very important in closing a sale, and prepayment means closing a sale.

In marketing a public seminar, you can take payment in the form of a check (no cash in the mail), money order, or credit card. Set up a merchant's credit-card account with the bank that handles your business checking account.

There are those who say they don't like to have participants pay with credit cards because the bank charges a fee for the service of processing charge cards. That's true, the bank will charge you a small percentage to handle the transaction. But the fee is small, and when I was conducting public seminars I was happy to pay this fee to the bank. Registration showed a marked increase when I made charge-card payment available to participants. I tracked the registration results based upon this credit-card method for a long time, and it remained a key factor in the number of registrants.

In developing your registration form, leave space for

Credit Card # _____ Type _____

Expiration Date _____

Your (participant's) Signature _____

as well as address and telephone number.

When the registration form arrives, transfer the information to a merchant's credit-card charge form (you can get those from your bank also). Clear the dollar amount on the telephone with the credit-card service number, deposit the charge forms, and you're finished. When you take a registration by mail, simply write "mail order" on the charge form, using the card holder's signature line. When taken by phone, write "phone order." The participants do not have to sign the forms themselves. Save the card holder copy and mail it back to the registrant with your confirmation form, or give it to him or her at check-in on the day of the seminar.

"800" TELEPHONE NUMBERS

At this point I'd like to mention the possibility of using an "800" telephone number. This is a number that allows your clients/participants to call you at no charge to them. It might be helpful to you if you are marketing outside your local area. Contact your local telephone company office for information.

FOREIGN PARTICIPANTS

If you will be having participants attending from foreign countries, make sure your price and registration form is clearly marked "U.S. Funds." (That is, if you are in the United States.)

REFUNDS, CANCELLATIONS, AND RESCHEDULING

If you are marketing public seminars, there will be times when someone cannot attend the seminar and wants a refund. You should decide if you want to have a no-refund policy, or offer to reschedule participation in a future seminar. This policy should be decided upon in advance of your communications so that if the occasion arises, you will know what to do. The majority of people who have to cancel their attendance at a public seminar will usually agree to reschedule. Whatever you decide to do about cancellations, refunds, and/or rescheduling (if appropriate), make a firm policy and stick to it. Then build a cost factor into your budget to help defray these expenses. It need not be a large amount, but don't ignore these factors altogether.

GROUP OR MULTIPLE DISCOUNT RATES

It is a good idea to have a small discount rate available for several people attending the seminar from one group. Just be careful that your scale for discounts makes sense in relation to your cost and budget. If you belong to an organization that is conducting the seminar, you may wish to have a member and nonmember rate.

If you are an S/T and you conduct and/or market seminars to a group (not public seminars), your billing system is a matter of personal preference. There are so many various ways of billing a client that my only advice is to be fair to yourself and to the client. There's nothing wrong with requiring a retainer for your preseminar work on their behalf—that's fair to you. Be fair to them by providing invoices and allowing time for their accounting departments to do their job.

In closing this section on communication with participants, I would like to suggest once again that you put yourself in the participant's place. Use the information in this section and be aware of the participant's needs—this will enable you to do a good job of the communication process.

Ask a Pro

Interview with:
Mr. Norman Levine
President, NORMAN LEVINE & ASSOCIATES
San Francisco, California

SHEILA: What advice would you give to someone new to the job of staging seminars?

NORMAN: I think that no one should attempt to run a seminar unless he or she has been present at, or participated in, the planning of another seminar under the direction of a pro. The second thing I strongly urge is that the entire proceeding be taped, properly taped, so that it can be used as a review, and records kept on the entire procedure and a file established so that the necessary corrections could be implemented with the next meeting, not from guesswork or memory, but from facts.

SHEILA: Is there a single most important item in staging a seminar?

NORMAN: If you're looking for a single item, I would be inclined to say the premeeting preparation. The careful arrangement of details in advance will help prevent major errors and mistakes during the seminar. For example, making sure that the participants in the seminar are aware of everything that's happening, such as room locations, their accommodations, what is expected of them, etcetera.

SHEILA: In staging seminars, what do you think is the most common mistake?

NORMAN: I feel the most frustrating thing is the specific room setup. Frequently, the rooms are too narrow, the head table is in the wrong place. The room should be set up so the speaker is as close to center as possible and the audience is funneled into the room to fill the center first and then the sides.

The other mistake is the lighting. Lighting is often inadequate or improperly directed. A spotlight may be too bright and blind the speaker so that he or she doesn't have eye contact. Or the lighting is misdirected and creates shadows so the speaker can't be clearly seen. Also, bright lights or windows behind the speaker are very distracting.

Another mistake is not having more than one microphone available. What often happens is that the microphone being used malfunctions and there is no backup system. It is very important to be sure that there is a secondary microphone ready to be used at moment's notice. It is also a good idea to have a backup speaker in case the primary speaker is late or doesn't show up.

SHEILA: Do you have a final comment you would like to make?

NORMAN: Yes. I think it's important that people organizing seminars not be afraid to do something different, to be creative in the planning and execution of the seminar. Be creative.

part four
THE SEMINAR

chapter twenty-four
ARRIVAL INFORMATION

The seminar is close at hand. You've done your advance work. You've communicated with the participants, and you have been in close touch with your suppliers and the seminar facility.

It is now preseminar time. A day or two before the seminar there are loose ends to tie up, some things that could not have been completed or taken care of before now.

Before leaving for the seminar facility, double-check to be sure you have all your materials, supplies, contracts, Handy Dandy Scout Box, shipping materials, and your planner's manual. In other words, take everything you could possibly need. Even in the most remote emergency it is better to have too much than not enough.

Here are some categories that have been discussed earlier in the book, and now need to be finished or executed; others in this list have not been mentioned before.

Your preseminar and day-of-seminar checklist will include the following headings:

PARKING AND LOADING AREAS

You may want to have a special parking spot where you or someone in your staff can load and unload equipment and supplies. Find out if there is a special entrance to your facility where you can more readily do this loading and unloading.

Does your facility have an awning that can be put up during inclement weather? If your seminar will take place at night, check the outside lighting around the facility. They may not always be aware of the fact that some of their lighting is not working. It is important for the safety of your participants.

NOTICE AND ANNOUNCEMENT BOARDS

When you first make contact with the facility, ask about their notice or announcement board. You may be able to have your company, group, or seminar name put on an outside announcement board that is visible from the street. Sometimes there is a small charge. Your budget will determine whether you care to do this. Inside there is usually a directory board of the events occurring in the facility. Check to be sure your seminar is properly listed.

DIRECTIONAL SIGNS

If the facility is large or laid out in an odd fashion, ask for stanchions (freestanding lobby signs) with your company, group, or seminar name posted and arrows pointing the way to your seminar room. It will help insure the participants' comfort, and your seminar will start on time. If you are using facilities that are spread out over a large area, with seminars in different rooms or buildings, you may need to put signs outside on trees, fences, posts, or gates. If you use a "hideaway" retreat or resort, you may even want to put locator/directional signs on the road to the facility. Use your imagination on these ideas.

chapter twenty-five
REGISTRATION

HOST-HOSTESSES-STAFF

The seminar speaker/trainer should avoid registering the participants. Enlist the help of staff or volunteers to act as host and hostesses. Or hire part-time staff to insure that the registration runs as smoothly as possible. There are temporary employment agencies in every city or town that can help you with people to do the registering. Quite often convention bureaus will have the names of these people.

Meet with your host/hostesses/staff prior to the seminar to explain what you expect of them and to delegate their responsibilities. A week in advance is ideal; however, if that is not possible, meet with them the day prior to the seminar. As a last resort, have them arrive one or two hours early.

If your seminar is to have over forty or fifty people in attendance or the facility is laid out in an odd fashion (where the registration is not readily available or cannot be seen easily), you may wish to have one host or hostess welcoming and directing the guests at the facility entrance.

At this point it seems appropriate to say a few words about the *attitude* of your host/hostess/staff. They are the most important people at the seminar before it actually begins. Choose only people who can smile easily and who are truly interested in making your guests feel welcome. I have seen people actually leave before the beginning of a seminar because of the lack of good attitude, courtesy, or efficiency on the part of the registration staff. No seminar leader should have to work at overcoming a poor welcome or ill feelings created at a registration table. When the registration goes smoothly the seminar leader can relax and get off to a strong, professional start.

LOCATION OF REGISTRATION TABLE

In setting up your check-in/registration table, review the size and shape of the seminar room itself. There are two schools of thought as to where the table should be placed. One is inside the room; the other is outside, in a hallway or foyer. Some locations will not allow your participants to crowd hallways or areas adjacent to the seminar room.

If you want an open, airy feeling, put the registration table outside of the seminar room; it gives the participants an extra feeling of welcome, and you will have the seminar room free for your refreshments, mingling, and socializing. Large groups will need the entire seminar room for comfortable seating and refreshment areas.

On the other hand, if the room is larger than you want, or the attendance is small and you want to fill up space or get the dialogue started early, having the registration table on the inside will help fill that vacant feeling and add to the initial hustle and bustle you want to build your active group dynamics. In his book *The Advance Man*, Jerry Bruno told how he would get a gymnasium or facility that seated only a few thousand people, when many thousands were expected to hear Senator John F. Kennedy's presidential campaign speeches. It would create the atmosphere of much larger crowds than were actually present.

TABLES AND CHAIRS

The standard five-foot (30-by-60-inch) table will comfortably accommodate two people sitting side by side in chairs for the registration. Other sizes available are six-foot (30-by-72-inch) and eight-foot (30-by-96-inch) tables.

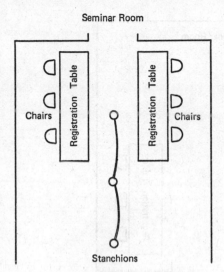

This set-up is for a long, narrow hall leading to
the seminar room.

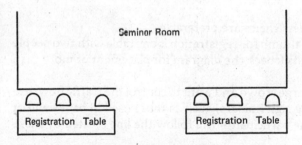

This set-up is for an open hallway or lobby area leading to the
seminar room.

The tables should be covered with floor-length coverings. Most facilities have a pleated skirt that attaches to the edge of the table over the tablecloth. This looks very attractive. Again, be sure that you ask for this; don't assume that they will automatically put it on. A side benefit of these floor-length skirts is that you can easily put supplies and materials under the table and keep a very neat and orderly registration area.

167

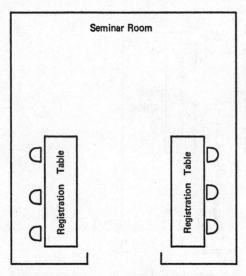

The seminar room can be any dimension.
This registration set-up will work either way.

Standard armless chairs are preferable.

A good rule of thumb for registration is one table with two people for every forty guests (check the diagram for placement of more than one table).

If you have a large crowd and want to control the traffic flow, use stanchions (standing sign holders) such as those used in banks and at sporting events. The participants will follow the line created by these stanchions.

Have separate tables for separate functions: e.g., one table for prepaid registrants and one for late registration.

FLOOR MATS

If it is raining or snowing outside, you may need a rug or mat of some sort at the entrance to prevent the guests from slipping on an uncarpeted floor, and also to protect the carpeting. This is a little item, but it can be very sloshy, wet, and dangerous if you forget.

168

SIGNS AND DIRECTIONS

Directional signs that are large and easy to read should be displayed to guide your guests to the proper check-in and registration location, using such titles as: Registration Table, Check-In Table, Advanced Registration, Pay Here, Name Tags, Seminar Materials, etc. At smaller events, all of this business can be covered at one stop with a sign posted to explain the process to participants. People feel more comfortable when they are sure they are in the correct line or at the proper location. These signs may be placed on the tables; however, it is much more effective if standing sign holders or room dividers (with signs attached) are used. In a pinch, a moveable chalkboard can be used with a little stickum gum to hold the signs or with the actual directions written on the board. These directions should be placed behind the registration table.

PARTICIPANTS' LIST

Have an alphabetically typed guest list, to be checked off as each participant arrives. The spelling of each name, business, and home telephone number should be verified from this list as he or she arrives. If the participants are not preregistered, have an "A through Z" list for the name, address, ZIP code, and telephone numbers for both business and home. It should be filled in by the host or hostesses (not the guests); this will insure more legibly printed information. If you have several people from a group or company, list the group or company alphabetically, then list the peoples' names below (this is easier than trying to find individual names at a later date).

A time-saving tip for your mailing list: As your guests arrive, register and verify the proper information, then type or print the information directly onto a mailing label—voilà! You are ready for your follow-up mailing.

PAYMENT AT REGISTRATION

If you accept payment at the time of registration, be sure to have all the items you will need, such as an imprinter for credit cards (you may wish to take deposit receipts along and make up your deposit at the seminar, particularly if the seminar lasts for several days).

If you accept cash, have change and a cash box available. Be sure to bring a receipt book.

NAME TAGS AND BADGES

There are several types of name tags or badges available. Self-adhesive (paper or fabric), pocket-inserted, pinned—all with or without colored borders. Your choice will depend on who you want to wear them. Sometimes there is a problem with the kind that attaches with a pin—it can damage clothing. So try the self-adhesive type in this case. There are some that have a standard "HELLO, MY NAME IS _____ ." For a nominal fee you can have a local printer imprint your organization's name, a slogan, or the seminar name on the badges or name tags. Your host/hostesses/staff should also have name tags that are easy to read. They should read "HOST" or "HOSTESS" or some other appropriate designation for your participants' comfort and convenience in recognizing them.

Participants' badges and name tags may be prepared in advance, when you have advance reservations. Some seminar leaders like to have them laid out on the table for the guests to find when they come in. This saves time at registration in hand writing the name tags.

A name tag or badge serves another important function. When guests pay at the door, the tag or badge is issued upon payment; the participants are not seated or allowed into the seminar without the badge or tag. In large events this will greatly help crowd control.

The items listed in "Day of" Communication Time Frame are given at this point also.

LATE REGISTRANTS

After the seminar has begun, have a sign that will direct and expedite the registration of late arrivals.

If your event will last for more than one day, or if people will arrive at different times for different events or seminars, you will need a permanent, centrally located area for all of your registration functions.

OVERNIGHT/OUT-OF-TOWN PARTICIPANTS

When participants are coming from out of town and/or they are staying overnight, be sure to have someone to:

- Accommodate their needs when they register.
- Help them become acquainted with the events, seminars, and their locations.
- Take them to their rooms and help them with their personal needs.
- Hand out agendas, explain the rules of the house and use of the locator map, and provide them with names of the staff to go to for help.

In seminars that will last more than one day, this has a major impact on your guests—positive or negative. If participants bring a spouse or guest, have a breakout room that can be used as a social gathering place for these guests while the participants are in the seminar.

This social room or rooms can display local information about the area: shopping, tours to take, or special events that are scheduled. With large groups of guests, have a staff member on duty full-time to care for their needs.

Ask a Pro

Interview with:
Mr. Richard Bolles
Director, NATIONAL CAREER DEVELOPMENT PROJECT
Walnut Creek, California

SHEILA: What advice would you give to someone new to the job of staging seminars?

RICHARD: Logistics are important, but they are secondary. In regard to the person conducting the seminar, the most important thing is to be as real as you possibly can with the seminar participants. If you are willing to step out of the role of "perfect person" and create a dialogue with the participants as human beings, this is more important than the staging.

Another factor is a sense of humor. It is the ability to take whatever and integrate it with the learning experience of the seminar.

SHEILA: Is there a single most important item in staging a seminar?

RICHARD: The things that I care greatly about are the size of the room and the placement of the chairs. I prefer the room to be rectangular in shape with the platform placed on the long wall, rather than setting up the room with the chairs in a long, narrow configuration. I always work from a platform at least a foot high so that my easel can be seen by everyone. If I'm working right down on the floor without a platform, it is crucial that my easel be raised high enough so that everyone can see.

Another important item, for me, is the darkness of the room. Since I work in the dark with overhead projectors, I look for a room that can be darkened enough so that the people can still take notes while viewing the screen. I also think the seminar leader must make sure the microphones are working properly. A dead "mic" can kill you, but the people will forgive you if you just talk openly about such a problem if it happens.

SHEILA: In staging seminars, what do you think is the most common mistake?

RICHARD: I go to a lot of seminars and a couple of mistakes I see people make that I think are crucial are: 1) When speakers write on blackboards or overhead projectors, they write so small that people can't possibly see what has been written. 2) When using an overhead projector, they keep it on stage with them, and the items they are projecting are so close to the screen that the images never fill the screen. Consequently, the people farther back are unable to see. I would suggest they have an assistant place the projector farther back in the room and have a signal or simply nod their head to go to the next slide or transparency. 3) People use unimaginative transparencies, forgetting that they can take a blank piece of paper and write on it in front of the group, thus having a dynamic movement to their presentation which is far more interesting to their participants. 4) When someone has a seminar that lasts more than one day, they should choose a facility that has inexpensive food sources within walking distance, for the participants' convenience.

SHEILA: Do you have a final comment?

RICHARD: Yes, I just want to be sure that a person planning a seminar has first of all grasped the importance of the overall concept of the seminar before worrying about staging and logistics. A bad seminar occurs when one thinks that staging and logistics are the greatest priorities in the planning.

chapter twenty-six
ROOM DETAILS

COATRACKS AND COATROOMS

During inclement weather, it is particularly handy and thoughtful to provide your participants with a place to hang their coats. Have rolling clothes racks that can be easily brought in and left at the back of the room. If you prefer not to have the coatrack in full view, use a divider screen or display screen to conceal it from the rest of the room. If your facility has a coatroom close to your seminar area, see if you can make arrangements to use it at no charge. Have a sign at the registration area informing the registrants that a coatrack or coatroom is available.

TABLES IN THE SEMINAR ROOM

There are several sizes and shapes of tables most commonly used. Most of them are folding and collapsible and easily moved. The format of your seminar, room size, and number of participants will determine which size and shape of table you use. The following are the most common types:

- Round tables—they will seat from four to ten people, depending upon the diameter

- Square tables—usually hold a maximum of four people comfortably
- Oval conference tables—are various sizes and are usually not of the folding type
- Rectangular five-, six- and eight-foot tables (30 by 60 inches, 30 by 72 inches, 30 by 96 inches respectively)
- Narrow rectangular tables (18 by 72 inches) are sometimes available.

Section II, Chapter 6—Seminar Room Set-Up Styles—discusses the use of these various tables.

Table Linens

Most facilities provide table linens at no additional cost. If you ask, you may have a choice of colors. In some of the finer hotels and facilities you may even find a selection of fabrics and patterns. Facilities do not usually volunteer this information, so the key is to ask.

CHAIRS

A standard armless chair is practical for most purposes. A word to the wise: If you are renting chairs from an outside source, *do not* trust them to bring the kind you want or that are in good condition. Go to the store, warehouse, or supplier facility and pick them out *yourself*.

If you are using an educational facility, the chairs with the attached writing arm will often be available. Check that the swinging operation of the writing arm is in working condition.

FLOOR SITTING

If your seminar style calls for a more casual seating arrangement, such as sitting on the floor, be aware of the fact that often the carpeting is put directly on top of concrete, at least on the ground floor of most facilities. This can be very hard and cold. For comfortable floor sitting, use a padded mat or pillow to sit on. A reed mat would do in a pinch, but it's far less desirable.

Have a firm surface for participants to hold in their laps for writing upon (magazine, seminar folder, or binder, for example).

SMOKING AND NONSMOKING

In arranging the room, I suggest that you have separate sections for smokers and nonsmokers. It is easy to put a small sign on each table designating smoking and nonsmoking. When the participants arrive they can be directed to the proper seating by an usher or a host/hostess. If the seminar is not large enough for ushers, inform the participants of the choice of tables. You may wish to inform them of the different sections on the literature you have mailed to them in your close-in communications. When housing people overnight or on weekends, be sure not to put smokers with nonsmokers. It is also a very nice courtesy to designate separate eating areas or dining areas for the comfort of your nonsmokers.

If the facility does not have air conditioning, try to put the smokers near the windows or doors. Don't put them across the room from the air source; it will draw the smoke through the nonsmokers. In a room that has air conditioning and a fan system, try to find out in advance if the air conditioner draws more heavily in one area than another. Ask the facility if they know; if not—and if you have time— turn the system on and experiment by having someone smoke a cigarette and watch the direction in which the smoke is pulled.

As a courtesy to the speaker/trainer, have the front section of the room designated for nonsmokers. It can be extremely uncomfortable for a speaker/trainer to have the smokers sitting right in front.

When having a facility set the room in advance, ask them to leave the ashtrays at the back of the room, then you can put them where you want them. A small room may not take much time to correct, if the ashtrays are in the wrong area; however, large groups take a lot of time to change.

SEMINAR-ROOM TEMPERATURE

I have walked into an empty seminar room set for 850 people and realized, to my horror, that the room was warm and comfortable. The participants were to arrive in one-half hour and there was no possible way to lower the room temperature in time.

You only have to go through watching 850 people fill a seminar room and within twenty minutes use their seminar materials as fans, to realize how important a factor room temperature can become.

The old idea of keeping people cool to keep their attention comes into play here. Sixty-eight degrees is a good temperature to start with. It is easier to warm a room than to cool it off. Have the facility set the temperature several hours in advance of the seminar. The control units in some facilities have locked covers on them, which means that frustration will set in if you discover that you want to change the temperature—and here is this little plastic box that you can see, but you can't get to, to work with the controls.

So put your room temperature on your facility advance checklist and save yourself a lot of stress.

EXITS

Most exits in facilities are well marked. However, you should review and check these with your staff. Also make sure that you know who is in charge of locking and unlocking these exits for fire safety or any emergency exit. (Review the material enclosed in this book from the National Fire Protection Agency. This material is found in Section II, Chapter 13—Fire Protection.)

MESSAGE BOX/BOARD

A message box or board is a must for seminars that last more than one day and can be helpful for those lasting only a few hours.

Incoming messages for participants, guests, or spouses; participant-to-participant messages; or program changes and/or announcements can be posted in or on the message box or board.

Place your message box or board in a convenient place and inform your participants of its use and location. Assign a staff member the responsibility for care and usage of the message box or board. Seminars lasting several days may need a mail-delivery arrangement. For a message board use a cork board with pins, chalkboard with tape, or, as a last resort, use a tabletop where messages can be taped.

PAGING SYSTEMS AND MUSIC

In a hotel or restaurant, check to be sure that the paging system is off before you begin the seminar. There is very little that is more disconcerting than having a page for Mr. or Mrs. so-and-so in the middle of the seminar. You may want to have the public address system music piped into the seminar room until just before the seminar begins. Most facilities must turn off the music and paging systems in order to turn the microphones on. This is a good safeguard. But be sure to coordinate this for a timely beginning of your seminar.

There are often control panels near the seminar room, and you may be able to perform this function yourself. Be sure to locate them in advance. Most facilities have staff to work the systems or to instruct you in their proper use.

If you take a cassette player along, with your own choice of mood music for background effect, place it next to the microphone and you can stop and start it at will. You have control and don't have to worry about the facility system.

FOOD AND REFRESHMENTS

If you arrive the day before the seminar, sit down with the catering manager and review every detail previously covered. If you arrive the day of the seminar, do this by telephone the day before; then when you arrive, meet with them in person for a last-minute check.

Be sure they understand when you want the refreshment breaks. If these breaks are to be served in the seminar room, arrange to have a staff member posted at the door a few minutes before the facility plans to bring them in. If the speaker/trainer is not quite ready to take the break, it can be very disturbing to have people walking in and out setting up refreshments. You may want to have some sort of signal with your speaker/trainer to tell you it is the right time to begin the break.

During the break the facility staff should come in and refill the pitchers of water on the tables. (Be sure you have made these arrangements well in advance.) When using a plate under the pitcher, have

177

them put a paper doily between the plate and pitcher. It will save a lot of clanking noises and will absorb the moisture from the melting ice so that it doesn't drip on notes and/or papers. Another idea for the water pitcher is to fill it one third with ice and the rest with water. Most facilities do just the opposite. Two problems arise when they do it that way: First, there is a lot of noise when a participant pours the water. (You would be surprised how noisy it can be when several people pour water at the same time.) Secondly, there is not enough water in the pitcher to go around. So people start pouring out the melted ice and the noise factor goes up 50 percent—or worse, they start chewing on the ice when the water is gone. Rarely has a catering person or setup crew sat through a seminar and had to endure these things, either as a participant or a speaker/trainer. It is not that they are thoughtless, they just don't understand.

During the coffee, Sanka, and tea breaks, be sure napkins and a wastebasket are around. A word to the wise—don't make your tea-drinking participants feel like second-class citizens by letting the facility forget to put out tea bags and lemon slices. You would be surprised at how many facilities don't realize that there are a lot of tea drinkers in the world.

As in all other sections of this book, make a detailed checklist, take it with you, and tend to the little matters as closely as you do the big ones.

LOST AND FOUND

Have a location and/or staff member designated for the lost-and-found area. Have a section of your message box or board for lost-and-found notices.

SPEAKER/TRAINER NEEDS

Even though you have done your homework for your speaker/trainer, there are some last-minute details: 1) If you have more than one speaker/trainer, be sure they have met and have had a chance to socialize. 2) Go over all the details of their presentation that they may need assistance with. 3) Review refreshment and/or food and the time frames in which they are served, the time to begin and the time to end, and what exactly is served and to whom. 4) Review room setup, such as stage, risers, and the front-of-the-room details with the speaker/trainer. 5) Review and test all audiovisual equipment with the S/T. 6) If the S/T will be using an overnight sleeping room or a changing room, be sure he or she is comfortable and has all personal needs tended to. 7) Review any special travel arrangements that the S/T may have.

A general rule would be to put yourself in the speaker/trainer's place. What would make you happy or comfortable if you were to conduct a seminar? Empathy is a great point of reference.

AUDIOVISUAL FINAL CHECK

Even though you will review the audiovisual equipment with your speaker at the time of his or her arrival, you need to check everything yourself first. Do you have replacement parts? Has your staff or the facility staff checked out the equipment? Don't depend on someone else other than you or your staff to do the final check of audiovisual equipment.

WORKING WITH THE SETUP CREW

I assume that by now you have provided the facility with diagrams of the registration area and seminar room. Now inquire as to when the setup crew will actually do their work. Inform the facility that you will have someone there just to make sure the crew understands. The facility will probably not like this idea. They may feel it is an insult or shows lack of confidence in them. Don't let them talk you out of it. Even if you or your staff have to get up at 4 A.M. or stay up until all hours of the night, be sure you are there during the setup.

You know exactly how you want that room to look. It is easier to make changes during the setup than to try to change it afterward.

SPEAKER/TRAINER WORKING AREA

Here are some ideas and items to use when preparing the front of the room and speaker/trainer area:

1. Head table—If you will be using a head table, have floor-length table-cloths or some kind of a modesty panel covering the front of the table. If you are using a tablecloth, be sure that the material is completely to the floor in front and try not to have too much of it in the laps of those sitting at the table. When you use a panel of speakers, consider having the lectern or person directing the panel positioned off to the side, rather than in the middle of the table. This will assist in better communications with the people at the table.

2. Work tables for the speaker/trainer—If it is necessary to have a table or work area of some kind in the speaking area, evaluate very carefully the size, shape, and placement of it. The area around the speaker can become too busy and will be a distraction to the participants. It may be better to have a table off to one side and an assistant to hand the speaker/trainer whatever is necessary.

3. If there will be several speakers in the work area at one time or if you are having a panel discussion, the best type of chair to use is one that is padded. If they will be sitting behind a table, a chair with arms is not necessary. However, if they are not behind a table and are in full view of the participants, use chairs with arms. The speakers will be much more comfortable and at ease.

4. Don't put the S/T work area in front of uncovered windows and doors.

Ask a Pro

Interview with:
Mr. Bart Hodges
Former President, NATIONAL ASSOCIATION OF LIFE UNDERWRITERS
Austin, Texas

SHEILA: What advice would you give to someone new to the job of staging seminars?

BART: Recognize the fact that all best-laid plans are subject to failure. So arrive at the facilities early; check all details thoroughly. Have a backup for everything possible—for instance, a replacement bulb for the projector, a standby microphone for the podium.

SHEILA: Is there a single most important item in staging a seminar?

BART: There is, at least, a single most important *action*, and that is adequate and thoughtful preparation made well in advance and fully communicated to *all* involved in the promotion and staging of the event.

First, the manager of the seminar facilities should know exactly what is required. To assure this, a conference with management should be held covering physical requirements (platform, microphones, room layout, lighting, refreshments, and so forth), supported (or followed up) with a memorandum and sketch. Full agreement on what management can and will do in regard to these requirements should be obtained.

I have several other items I would like to mention, as they all contribute greatly to the overall success of the seminar.

1. Unless there is a head table, such as at a noon meeting, the speaking platform should be free of all items except what the speaker needs to present the seminar. A panel may require several people to be on the stage at the same time; otherwise, let the speaker be the sole attraction.

2. Encourage the speaker to use a lavaliere microphone and move away from the podium. This promotes contact between speaker and audience.

3. If the room is sufficiently large, have it darkened slightly and place a soft spotlight on the speaker. Above all, the speaker's face should be clearly seen. A lot can be said and communicated through facial expressions.

4. Don't have the speaking platform unnecessarily high. You want to prevent front-row attendees from having to bend their necks uncomfortably.

5. Check the microphone and sound system in advance, so that everything is working properly and so there are no spots in the room that produce microphone feedback.

6. If a failure occurs during the seminar, learn to interject some levity and keep the program participants and audience at ease. Try not to display impatience.

7. When you have a speaker who talks too long and goes over the time frame, have a signal from the back of the room that will get his or her attention to indicate the time is up.

8. Pray a lot!

SHEILA: In staging seminars, what do you think is the most common mistake?

BART: I think one of the most common mistakes is having a room that is too large for the size of the audience. Chairs are often placed to fill the room and then the audience scatters. It's always an uphill fight to produce a successful seminar under these conditions. I think it best to have a room set for slightly fewer than the number of people expected, then chairs can be added as more people arrive. Adding chairs conveys the impression of a very successful meeting. Most speakers and participants never seem to mind, just as they are never offended by the interruption of applause.

In the case where the room is larger than needed, I suggest that a seminar setup be as tight as practical and as close to the speaker's platform as possible. If the facility is an oversize theater-auditorium type, the staff should endeavor to achieve a compact audience by roping off the back sections and posting "guards" to keep people from sitting there.

It is always my intent to promote intimacy and friendliness, resulting in a more receptive and responsive audience, by seating people close together.

SHEILA: Do you have a final comment?

BART: That all your personal assistants (or committee members) be fully informed of their individual responsibilities.

For large meetings, I like to appoint a vice-chairman of "Things," such as printing of tickets and brochures, seating, staging, lighting, sound system, etcetera. I also have a vice-chairman of "People," which includes everything directly involving people.

If the chairman does his or her job properly, all duties will be delegated and he or she needs only to supervise, troubleshoot, and keep things moving according to plan.

part five
EVALUATION, FOLLOW-UP, AND DEBRIEFING

chapter twenty-seven
EVALUATION BY PARTICIPANTS

Whew! The seminar is over. All your hard work has come to fruition. Are you pleased with the results? Did you see some glaring errors that must be corrected before your next seminar?

It is now time for evaluation, follow-up, and debriefing.

Many seminar coordinators tend to just collapse after a seminar. They pack up and go home. That is an understandable reaction. However, there are things that need to be done, a few more details to be attended to.

Don't let down just yet. Your learning cycle is not quite complete. Your professional image needs some finishing touches.

There are two areas of evaluation to consider: One is the evaluation by the participants; the other is evaluation by you and your staff. Let's look at evaluation by the participants first.

There are varying opinions as to when you should ask your seminar participants to evaluate the seminar. Some say at the immediate conclusion of a seminar, right on the spot. Others think that sometime in the near future is best. Either way, here is a sample questionnaire.

SEMINAR LOGISTICS QUESTIONNAIRE

Dear Seminar Participant,

We would appreciate your opinions and feelings about the staging and logistics of this seminar. With your help, we will grow and improve. Please give us a rating on the following categories: (Circle a number)

	Excellent	Good	Average	Fair	Poor
1. Geographical location and area?	5	4	3	2	1
2. Facility overall?	5	4	3	2	1
3. Facility layout?	5	4	3	2	1
4. Sleeping rooms?	5	4	3	2	1
5. Food and refreshments?	5	4	3	2	1
6. Facility staff?	5	4	3	2	1
7. Travel arrangements?	5	4	3	2	1
8. Travel information?	5	4	3	2	1
9. Seminar staff?	5	4	3	2	1
10. Our communications with you prior to the seminar?	5	4	3	2	1
11. Our check-in registration system?	5	4	3	2	1
12. Seminar room setup?	5	4	3	2	1
13. Audiovisual presentation?	5	4	3	2	1
14. Seminar time frames (starting time, refreshment time, ending time)?	5	4	3	2	1

Was there anything that you felt was particularly good or bad (in regard to the staging and logistics of this seminar) that you would care to comment on? _____

_____

_____

_____

Any other comments? _____

_____

_____

Thank you for your help!

Please put today's date: _____

Please sign your name, if you wish: _____

_____

If you wish to, you may add questions that will give you feedback on the seminar, theme and objectives, format and design, content and presentation style.

If the participants are presented with a questionnaire that is easy to read and simple to respond to, they will share their opinions with you. Of course, there will always be those few individuals who either treat it like a joke or consider it their one chance to vent negative reactions and emotions. (These may have nothing to do with you or your seminar.)

Putting those aside, most people will be candid with you, especially if they can omit their signatures. The questionnaire should have as many questions as you feel necessary to give you proper feedback.

chapter twenty-eight
EVALUATION BY YOU AND YOUR STAFF

There are two times to have a staff evaluation. The first is immediately following the seminar. After the participants have left, you and your staff should adjourn to a quiet place and verbally share reactions, feelings, and opinions. This is an informal get-together to wrap up the event. An emotional vacuum can be created if everyone just scatters at the seminar conclusion. (A formal debriefing will be held later.) This meeting gives you and your staff an opportunity to congratulate yourselves for your hard work. If the seminar did not turn out well, and there are negative feelings, you need to find something to praise your staff for. The problems and negative aspects can be discussed later. At the very least, your staff should be thanked for their efforts. (Even if they did not achieve the desired results, they did try.)

Then, within two or three days following the seminar, ask for a written evaluation from each staff member, including yourself. Here are some areas that need evaluation (and discussion at the debriefing session later):

- How did they feel about the overall and individual delegation of tasks?
- How did they feel about the communication system used among themselves—checklists, flow charts, etc.?
- What did they observe about the participants' reactions and response to their tasks (those and other tasks that they were not involved with)?

- How did they feel about the facility and its staff?
- What ideas do they have for future seminars?
- What was the best thing they did or were involved in during the planning, preparation, or execution of the seminar? What was the worst thing?
- What were their personal expectations? Were they fulfilled? Are they satisfied with their own work? How do they feel about the seminar in general?

A copy of each of these evaluations—participants' and staff's—should be included in your planner's manual. Another copy should be made for each staff member to use at the debriefing session.

The final step before you can conduct a debriefing session is to complete your follow-up procedures.

chapter twenty-nine
FOLLOW-UP AND DEBRIEFING

FOLLOW-UP

Your follow-up procedures will include such things as:

- Participants' evaluation forms.
- Final payments to facilities and suppliers.
- Refunds to or rescheduling of participants.
- Return of items in lost and found, if possible.
- Gratuities or gifts to suppliers or facility staff deserving of recognition for "above and beyond" service or effort during the seminar.
- Thank-you notes to suppliers, facility staff (individually if possible), your own staff, and participants. (Everyone involved should have a thank-you note.)

The final task for follow-up is collation of all your paperwork. Final submission of receipts for payments, evaluations, staff paperwork—everything that happened from conception through evaluation should be filed in your planner's manual. When this is completed (hopefully no later than a week or ten days after the seminar), you can then complete your final task, which is debriefing.

DEBRIEFING

When you met with your staff immediately following the seminar, you received their emotional reactions and observations. Then, with a little time and distance between them and the seminar, they wrote a formal evaluation (of which you have made copies for each of them). It is now time for your debriefing session.

If at all possible, get away from your daily surroundings. Find a quiet place to hold the session, free of distraction and interruption. Allow as much time as possible for the session, so members feel that they can express themselves and be freely heard.

What do you do at a debriefing session? As a seminar coordinator, it is your responsibility to have a flexible written agenda with a copy for each staff member. Begin the session with a positive thought, observation, or comment, and then open the session for the discussion period. Don't immediately give your own opinions and feelings, other than a positive opening statement. You may intimidate your staff by assuming a dominant role. Act as a facilitator. You have with you the complete planner's manual. You can, at any time during the discussion, turn to a section and provide answers to questions or information to clarify a situation or problem.

Discuss the entire seminar process, from your initial brainstorming session through the actual seminar to the follow-up tasks. With a free-flowing discussion based upon the planner's manual and the staff's personal experience and the evaluation questionnaires, you will be able to reconstruct the whole seminar process. You can share and learn from each other. You will be well prepared for your next seminar.

As seminar coordinator, summarize the session and leave each member with a verbal and perhaps physical pat on the back. You may even want to send out a final debriefing summary for each to keep in his or her file. The members' attitude about the seminar, about you, and about each other is vital. A happy and excited beginning of a new seminar will depend on these final feelings. If they can say, "Whew—it's over, we made some mistakes, we learned a lot, and had a good time," the next time you approach them—be it next week, next month, or next year—and say, "Let's have a seminar," you will receive a positive response.

Ask a Pro

Interview with:
Mr. Paul J. Meyer
President, SMI, INTERNATIONAL, INC.
Waco, Texas

SHEILA: What advice would you give to someone new to the job of staging seminars?

PAUL: I think the advice I would give to someone staging seminars would be twofold:

1. Whether you are staging a seminar for yourself or someone else, be sure that you know exactly what you want your seminar to accomplish and be sure you know what audience you wish to appeal to.

2. Leave no detail uncovered. Once you know what you plan to accomplish and what audience you plan to reach, the balance is a matter of detail. There is no detail too small for the seminar planner's attention. The checklist has to be constructed and gone over many, many times.

SHEILA: Is there a single most important item in staging a seminar?

PAUL: Yes. I think the single most important item is to be clear on the objective that you want the seminar to accomplish. If you know what you plan to accomplish as a result of your seminar, then the facilities, agendas, locations, etcetera are much easier to select since everything you select will enhance that objective.

SHEILA: In staging seminars, what do you think is the most common mistake?

PAUL: I think the most common mistake is that too many people try to get one seminar to accomplish too many objectives. I think for a seminar to be good it can accomplish only one major objective. There can be secondary benefits, but the seminar should be planned to accomplish only the single objective. Too many seminars are produced to appeal to too many different audiences simultaneously.

SHEILA: Do you have a final comment?

PAUL: I found that people look to seminars for information and inspiration. But the seminars very rarely contribute to long-term growth. I think what contributes to people's long-term growth is a method of consistently reinforcing their attitudes and skills through repetitive exposure to ideas and, even more importantly, clearly defined goals that they are willing to commit themselves and their abilities to. In SMI we have tried to combine the best of both: the seminars to inform and inspire people, and a personal-goals program to help them define their goals and commit to their accomplishment. Both of these are then supported by the repetitive exposure to positive ideas. It is a unique concept in that it provides motivation, goal setting, and skill development. We feel a person needs all three to continue to grow.

part six
WHERE ELSE CAN I GET HELP?

chapter thirty
RESOURCES

Before you can plan your seminar, you need as much information as possible on who else can help you with a specific problem. There are specialists who have knowledge and experience in nearly every area you will encounter in planning a successful seminar. Why not cut down on your learning curve, save yourself some time and a lot of trouble? Here's a list of ideas on whom to contact and what services or help they can offer you. This is by no means a complete list; however, someone on this list will be able to answer a question you may have on a more specific matter.

Meeting Planners International (MPI)

Address:	3719 Roosevelt Boulevard
	Middletown, Ohio 45042
	Attention: Manager of Education
Telephone:	(513) 424-6827
Service:	They publish a resource book which lists all books and articles published on the subject of meeting planning, updated annually. Also publishers of *Directory of Supplier Members and Planner Members*. This directory will give you the names of all the Meeting Planners International membership, including both people who plan meetings and supply services for the meetings.

International
Association of Convention
and Visitors' Bureaus (IACUB)

Address: 702 Bloomington Road
                Champaign, Illinois 51820
Telephone: (217) 359-8881
Service: They produce a general information and membership di-
                rectory, comprising over one-hundred member bureaus
                worldwide.

Convention and visitor bureaus are extremely helpful in planning any
kind of a seminar of any size in any part of the country. Most bureaus
have the names of people who specialize in or can provide clerical or
other services in the areas you may need.

Johnson's World-Wide
Chambers of Commerce Directory

Address: Johnson Publishers, Inc.
                P.O. Box 455
                Eighth Street and Van Buren
                Loveland, Colorado 80537
Telephone: (303) 667-0652
Service: This is a directory of chambers of commerce worldwide. If
                you call directly to the publisher, they can provide this
                directory for you. The U.S. Public Library carries this
                book, catalogued in the Dewey decimal system as follows:

                REF-381
                w893
                This directory is updated in July of each year.

Hotel Sales Management
Association International (HSMA)

Address: Publication Office
                333 N. Gladstone Avenue
                Margate, New Jersey 08402
Telephone: (609) 823-1979

Service:	They publish the official hotel and motel directory and facilities guide, a basic guide for the user of hotel and motel facilities. It is published annually and provides comprehensive information about hotels and motels all over the world.

American Society
of Training and Development (ASTD)

Address:	600 Maryland Avenue, S.W. Washington, D.C. 20024
Telephone:	(202) 484-2390
Service:	This society publishes a cross-reference of information in the field of training and development, called the *Buyers' Guide*. This contains helpful information for any number of concerns connected with seminar planning and implementation. You can obtain a copy by contacting their office.

National Speakers' Association

Address:	5201 North 7th Street Phoenix, Arizona 85014 Attention: Executive Director
Telephone:	(602) 265-1001
Service:	This is an association of speakers and trainers, whose subjects cover a wide range of topics. You will probably find the speaker/trainer and topic you need. Contact them for a copy of their directory of members. They are not a speakers' bureau and will not recommend a speaker/ trainer to you, but the directory will give you an excellent choice of speaker/trainers to contact for your research throughout the United States and in several foreign countries.

American Society
of Association Executives (ASAE)

Address:	1575 Eye Street, N.W. Washington, D.C. 20005

Telephone: (202) 626-2723
Service: Each year this association publishes an updated edition of
                    a directory entitled *Finding the Right Speaker*. They contact
                    and include speakers and trainers on a wide variety of
                    topics. You may contact them for a copy of the directory.

American Society
of Travel Agents (ASTA)

Address: 711 Fifth Avenue
                    New York, New York 10022
                    Attention: Vice-President, Member Services
Telephone: (212) 486-0700
Service: This society will provide a membership roster to assist you
                    in selection of an agent in any city or region.

Association
of Retail Travel Agents (ARTA)

Address: Eight Maple Street
                    Croton-on-Hudson
                    New York, New York 10520
                    Attention: Membership Director
Telephone: (212) 299-5151
                    (914) 271-9000
Service: They make available a printout of members in a specific or
                    general area for travel assistance.

Successful Meetings Magazine

Address: Circulation Department
                    633 Third Avenue
                    New York, New York 10017
Service: This is a monthly magazine that includes two special
                    annual directories as a part of the subscription; they are
                    also available for purchase separately: *International Conven-
                    tion Facilities Directory* and *Sites '81* (annual update)—*A Direc-
                    tory of Cities and Areas for Meetings and Trade Shows*.
                    The *International* directory provides information on specific
                    hotels and their facilities. The *Sites* directory gives detailed

information and background on various cities. The combination of these two directories gives an overall picture of an area and the facilities available to you.

Meetings and Conventions Magazine

Address:	Circulation Department One Park Avenue New York, New York 10016
Service:	This is another monthly magazine that includes a special annual directory with subscription, or it can be purchased separately:

Gavel 1981 (annual update) *Annual International Directory.* This directory provides information on hotels, convention halls, and bureaus, city and resort location information, speakers and entertainers, transportation options, and sections on trade-show services of all types.

World Convention Dates Magazine

Address:	79 Washington Street Hempstead, New York 11550
Telephone:	(516) 483-6881
Service:	*World Convention Dates* has several services you can take advantage of:

1. They publish a monthly magazine that gives the who, what, when, and where of 28,000 events around the world. They list the type of event and the place and time. This will be very helpful when you want to see what else will be happening in a geographical area you wish to use for your seminar.

2. They publish an annual *Event Planners' Guide*. This gives information on site selection, services available, and professional speakers and trainers.

3. If you wish to publicize your seminar, they will do so at no charge if you contact them a minimum of three months prior to the seminar date. They will include your seminar in their list of events.

Your Local Library

Service:	Your local library contains a wealth of information on all aspects of seminar planning and implementation. I hope that you will spend time learning to use this valuable resource. It is all there for the taking. The only cost to you is a library card!

Suppliers
in the Specific Location
of Your Seminar

Service:	In most major cities you can go to the main office of the telephone company and use the directories they keep on hand, which cover the entire United States. Suppliers include:

> Audiovisual companies
> Catering services
> Equipment rentals
> Moving companies
> Car rental agencies
> Local airlines sales managers
> Part-time employment services

Your specific seminar needs determine the suppliers you will require.

Others Who Have Done It

Service:	Be sure to use the resources available to you in your own organization. Other people who have conducted seminars or workshops such as yours can be invaluable to you in shortcutting all the time and effort involved in seminar planning and avoiding costly mistakes. You can also tap the resources in related organizations outside your particular group, linking up with other seminar planners to take advantage of the successful practices they have used. Don't be shy about revealing that this is your first seminar or that you have a problem and would like their help. Most people are very happy to give assistance to someone else who is trying to do something they have already had experience in doing.

This chapter on resources will have given you a general idea of the types of things available to you in your problem-solving efforts and in the initial planning stages of your seminar.

AUDIO CASSETTE TAPES NOW AVAILABLE

Make the Most of Your Travel, Waiting and Spare Time!!

Professional speaker and trainer, Sheila Murray has over eight years experience conducting seminars. She has found that the learning process is greatly enhanced when auditory input accompanies the written word.

A six-pack audio cassette tape program is available as supplement to this book. It is packaged in book style in a vinyl cover to carry or put on the book shelf.

Recorded by the author, these cassette tapes are not a verbal transcription of this book. They contain concepts, ideas, and discussions that will add to the successful implementation of the material in this book.

Retail price of $75 Includes shipping and handling. (California residents add $4.88 sales tax).

Order by check or credit card. (Visa or Mastercard)
Credit card information:

Type of card: _____ Number: _____

Expiration Date: _____

Mail your order to:

Sheila L. Murray, President
Getting Control Inc.
1390 Market Street, # 908
San Francisco, CA 94102

or call
(415) 931–4507

INDEX

202